FAVOURITE ASSEMBLIES FOR AGES 4-7

Edited by Anne Stewart OBE

pfp

First published in this form in Britain in 2002 by
pfp publishing limited
61 Gray's Inn Road
London WC1X 8TH

Reprinted 2002
Reprinted 2003

Written by Gerald Haigh.
Illustrations by Sue Woollatt of GCI and Angela Lumley.
Cover and layout by Creative Media.
Cover photo by Getty Images/Photodisc.
Page design by Starfish.

Other assembly titles available from pfp include

- ***Favourite Assemblies for Ages 7–11***
- ***Assemblies for Sensitive Issues***
- ***The Primary Assembly Song Book***
- ***All Year Round – Assemblies for Special Days and Celebrations***
- ***Primary Assembly File***

pfp orders and customer service
Tel: 0870 241 0731
Web: www.pfp-publishing.com

Printed in the UK

ISBN 1 874050 55 4

A catalogue record for this book is available from the British Library.

CONTENTS

INTRODUCTION

The 40 assemblies in this collection have been carefully selected by Anne Stewart OBE for use with younger children aged between 4 and 7 years and are divided into the following common primary assembly themes.

- Abilities and achievements
- Differences and respecting others
- Myself
- How do I feel about that?
- My family
- Community and belonging
- Change
- Teamwork
- Thinking of others
- Awe and wonder

Taken from the *Primary Assembly File* subscription – a termly publication providing 60 brand new assemblies every year – these assemblies are the very best, all-time favourites from the entire collection.

Using the assemblies

Our assembly books are intended to support busy heads and teachers. They do this by providing you with assemblies which

- are easy to use
- tell stories that young children can enjoy
- carry serious spiritual messages.

You can use the assemblies in this book exactly as they are with very little preparation. Or, if you do have the time, then even a few minutes of preparation will make you more confident and allow you to adapt them to your own particular needs.

Good prior knowledge of an assembly means that you can

- pause for questions or discussion
- use poetry that you have chosen
- use children's writing or artwork
- set up simple role plays
- use periods of reflective silence
- tell the story in your own words
- edit the whole assembly for length or emphasis.

Each assembly begins with an introduction which leads into the main theme. Extra resources are clearly listed and only include items that are readily available in school.

The core of each assembly is a story or poem. These are self-contained, and you can easily use them on their own, incorporating them into your own way of working. This is specially helpful in schools where the time available for assembly is very short.

Links to Bible stories are made where appropriate and those who prefer a stronger Christian approach find that they can build our stories into daily acts of worship. Finally, each assembly finishes with a prayer or a thought and some song suggestions.

However you use them, you will find that they are stimulating, well written and valuable and that they work with the children in your school.

First steps

Assembly 1 of 4

This is an assembly about being able to do things. It looks at things children can and can't do. Some the children will learn to do; others will remain out of reach. The story is about a baby learning to walk.

You will need

- a blank OHT and a pen.

Taken by ....

Date ....

Given to ....

Comments

- ....
- ....
- ....

✦ Activity

Can you touch the sky? Let's reach up and see if we can touch the sky. Come on. Reach up everybody! Is anybody touching the sky?

Can you see the air around you? I can feel it if I wave my hand, can you? If I wave a hanky, the air makes it flap. But can we see it? Let's stare and stare around and see if we can see the air. Come on, everybody, really stare.

Could you hold the rain in your hands? A bit of it perhaps, but not very much.

Could you walk up the wall and across the ceiling? I don't think so. Perhaps we could pretend we can do that. We're walking across the hall floor. Now we're walking up the wall. It's quite hard, so we're going quite slowly.

(Optional) Now we're walking along the ceiling. It's making us a bit giddy.

Be careful with the lights, and the PE apparatus. We don't want to trip over it!

Right, we're across the ceiling. Now we're going down the other wall. Try not to run. Go slowly. One last step and here we are on the floor again.

Did you enjoy that trip?

There are lots of things we can't do. Some things we will be able to do one day. Some things we won't be able to do. We won't reach up and touch the sky. We won't catch all the rain. We won't see the air, no matter how hard we stare. We won't walk up the wall and across the ceiling.

But think of the things we can do now that we couldn't do once.

Who can think of something they can do now, that they couldn't do before?

Write on the OHT. Suggestions might include: read, write, do a forward roll, walk, skip...

Here's a story about someone who did something for the very first time.

First steps

Story

Karen was having her tea. Her dad was sitting opposite her. He wasn't saying very much. Her little sister Sarah was sitting in her high chair between them. She was saying a lot. She was gurgling and laughing and saying 'dada' and 'mama'. Every now and again, Karen's dad reached across and gave Sarah a spoonful of mashed up food.

Karen was used to her dad being quiet at teatime. He was always tired after work. Karen wasn't sure what her dad did, but he worked hard and came in every evening at six o'clock. When he came in, Karen's mum went out. She worked at the motorway service station. A minibus picked her up at a quarter past six and brought her back after Karen had gone to bed.

'I think Sarah wants some more, Dad. Can I give her some?' Karen asked.

'OK, Karen, you take over for a bit, while I go and get washed,' her dad replied.

Later on, Karen and her dad gave Sarah a bath. Sarah loved it and Karen liked to help. She poured warm water on Sarah's back, and Sarah laughed and screamed.

After her bath, Sarah lay on a towel on her mum and dad's bed with no clothes on. She kicked her little legs and waved her arms, and she laughed at Karen and her dad.

Karen tickled Sarah, and her dad kept talking to her in his special baby voice, 'Who's a lovely girl? Who's Daddy's lovely girl then?'

Together they put Sarah's nappy on and her pyjama suit and tucked her up in her cot. They kissed her goodnight and went downstairs.

When they were sitting down in the living room, Karen thought of something.

'Dad,' said Karen, 'when will Sarah be able to walk?'

'Not long now. She keeps pulling herself up on the chair and standing there. You've seen how she laughs when she does that. Soon she'll let go and walk across the room. That's what you did,' her dad replied.

Karen thought for a bit. 'I suppose I couldn't walk once,' she said.

'That's right. I remember when you walked for the first time. We were on holiday in Newquay, in a caravan. We were sitting outside the caravan and you were playing on the grass. You pulled yourself up on your mum's chair, and then you let go with one hand. Your mum said, "Go on, Karen. Go to your dad!" and you let go and tottered across to me. It was really good!' he said. Karen's dad smiled to himself at the memory.

'It won't be long before Sarah's off,' he said.

Most of the time, Sarah crawled around. She was really good at crawling. She could get up on all fours and just about run around – a bit like a guinea pig or a gerbil, thought Karen. When she was outside, she would get really dirty from crawling, and everybody had to watch her because she would find things on the floor and sometimes put them in her mouth. Once she picked a worm up from the lawn, and her dad jumped up from the garden seat so quickly that the chair went over. He galloped over to Sarah shouting, 'No! No! Put it down, Sarah!'

Sarah had just laughed, but luckily she didn't eat the worm.

Karen went to bed not long after Sarah. Her dad tucked her in and kissed her goodnight and then went to watch the television. Karen could hear the television faintly through the floor of her bedroom. It didn't disturb her, in fact it was quite comforting, because she knew her dad was there watching it.

First steps

She went to sleep quite quickly. Once, she half woke up. Her bedroom door opened for a moment, and her mum looked in and whispered goodnight.

Next morning, Karen was having breakfast with her mum before she went to school. 'Dad says that Sarah will be walking soon,' she said.

'She will that! Then we'll have to watch her. She'll be into everything!' replied her mum.

'Was I into everything?' Karen asked.

'Oh yes! We had to put everything out of your way – all my ornaments and pictures. Not for long, though. I taught you which things you could touch and which you had to leave alone. You were a good girl then. But you're a big Naughty Girl now!' said her mum.

Karen looked at her mum, but her mum was laughing, so Karen knew that it was a joke. Her mum leaned across and gave her a kiss.

'Come on now. It's Paula's turn to take you to school today. You'd better be ready,' she said.

At school, Karen kept thinking about Sarah. Karen really wanted to see Sarah walking for the first time. 'Suppose she walks for the first time while I'm at school!' thought Karen. 'I'll miss it!'

She didn't want to miss it.

That evening, Karen's mum got the tea ready as usual before she went out, and her dad came in on time at six o'clock. Karen's mum kissed her and went out of the door, and her dad put Sarah in her high chair ready for tea.

After tea, Karen and her dad played with Sarah on the big bed. 'Can we play downstairs for a bit?' asked Karen. Sometimes they did that. It was a bit of a treat for Karen and Sarah – their dad really liked to be peaceful when he was tired and sometimes he said no.

Tonight, though, he didn't mind. 'Right. We'll just put her nappy and vest on and I'll carry her down. You go and get her bricks out on the carpet.'

Sarah liked to sit on the carpet with Karen and play with her big bricks, while her dad watched TV. Soon they were all downstairs. Karen was building a big tower with the bricks, and Sarah was trying to knock it down. Her dad was starting to doze off as he usually did.

After a while, Sarah got fed up with the bricks, and crawled away across the room. She got to the table and pulled herself up. Then she stood there holding on and looking at Karen and laughing.

Karen sat quite still and held her hands out to Sarah. 'Come on, Sarah! Come to me! Come on!' she said.

Sarah laughed again and let go of the table with one hand.

'Come on then! Walk to Karen! Come on!' Karen repeated.

Sarah let go of the table with her other hand. She stood there swaying a bit.

'Dad!' whispered Karen. 'Look!'

They both looked without speaking as Sarah stood smiling and looking at them. Then she suddenly sat down with a bump.

'Oh dear!' said Karen.

But Sarah hadn't finished. She pulled herself up again. Just then, they heard the front door open and close, and who should come into the living room but their mum.

'Hello! Big power cut at the service station. They've sent us home. What...' she began.

Karen's dad was saying 'Shh' and pointing at Sarah. Karen's mum stood very still.

First steps

'Come on, Sarah!' said Karen again, holding her hands out.

Sarah took her hands off the table again. This time, though, she didn't waste time standing there. She set off and walked right across the carpet, waving her arms at the side to keep her balance and looking as if she was concentrating very hard.

When she got to Karen, she held her arms out, and Karen held on to them. Karen laughed and Sarah laughed. Sarah knew she had done something special and she looked really pleased with herself.

Karen's mum came over and picked Sarah up and cuddled her. Karen's dad laughed and he cuddled Karen.

'Sarah walked for the first time,' said Karen. 'And we were all there to see it! That's good, isn't it?'

'That's very good!' said her dad. 'Very good indeed, I would say!'

✦ Conclusion

It's always a big thing when a baby takes its first step or says its first word. There are all kinds of first things like that – the first time you ride a bike, the first time you buy something in a shop,the first day in school. Perhaps the first step is the most important though.

I wonder how old babies are when they walk for the first time. Does anybody know? Well the answer is that some babies walk earlier and some walk later. I suppose the earliest is about ten months, but some are well over a year old. Some babies get so good at crawling or scooting around on their bottom that they don't really want to hurry to walk. But eventually they get up and off they go.

Now you've thought of some of the things you couldn't do but you can do now.

Let's think of things you can't do yet and will be able to do in the future. Shall we make a list?

Write on the OHT. Suggestions might include driving a car, flying a plane, getting married...

A prayer

Dear God, we thank you for each thing we learn to do. We think of babies learning to walk and talk. We think of people learning in school, or in the home. We think of people starting out in new jobs or in new homes or new countries. Life is full of new things, and we ask for your help in meeting them. Amen.

A thought

Let's think of baby Sarah taking her first step. Let's think of all the things we can do now, and all the things we have to do in the future. We'll do them with the help of our families and friends.

Song suggestions

'Mysteries', *Tinder Box*, 40
'One more step', *Come and Praise*, 47
'The journey of life', *Someone's Singing Lord*

Optional follow up

Write the words 'I am a person who likes...' and then make a list of all the things you like, and the things you like to do.

Then write 'I am a person who does not like...' and make a list of all the things you don't like and the things you don't like to do.

Stick your lists together, and put a photograph of yourself with them.

George signs a card

Assembly 2 of 4

In this assembly a child reflects on the nature of writing and the meaning of marks on the page – she can write, her baby brother can make marks.

You will need

- a blank OHT and a pen.

Taken by ....

Date ....

Given to ....

Comments

- ....
- ....
- ....

✦ Introduction

This assembly is about writing. We learn reading and writing together – the more we write, the more it helps us with our reading, and the more we read, the more it helps us with our writing.

On the blank OHT make marks which start by being random, but which gradually transform into writing.

Look at these marks on the OHT. What's the difference between these at the beginning and these at the end?

Yes, the ones later on mean something, don't they? You can read them. These here are just marks. These later on are writing. Yet they are all marks on the page.

It's like talking – voice sounds without meaning are babble. When they start to mean something, the babble becomes talking.

Writing is nothing more than marks on the paper arranged in a special way. Sounds easy when you say it like that, but it takes a long time to learn, as you all know.

Writing carries messages from your brain, sometimes to yourself – a shopping list is a message to yourself – but usually it is to someone else.

Sometimes these messages are quite long – a story is a long message. Sometimes, there are short messages, but that does not mean that they are not important. A very short message can be very important indeed. If you write 'With love' on someone's present, that can be a very important message – it tells someone you love how much you think of them.

Being able to write simple messages to the people you love is a good reason for learning to write.

In our story we will meet Rachel, who can write a message to her dad on his birthday, and little George, who is a bit young for writing, but has a try nevertheless.

George signs a card

Story

'Don't forget your dad's card,' said Rachel's mum.

'We'll write it tonight when you get home from school. You know how much your dad likes to get a birthday card from you.'

Rachel thought all day about writing her dad's card. She knew exactly what she was going to put on it. 'To the best dad in the world, from Rachel.'

She had been putting that ever since she was old enough to be able to write. And each time it was her dad's birthday he would come down to breakfast and find his cards on the table, and he would really enjoy opening them and looking to see what was written in them.

So that evening, after tea, she settled down at the kitchen table with her card and a pencil. It was a nice card. She had chosen it herself and it had a picture of a man a bit like her dad, washing up in the kitchen with an apron on. She thought it was funny, and she thought her dad would like it.

She picked up her pencil and wrote the words. She finished off, 'With lots of love,' and she wrote quite a lot of kisses across the bottom.

'Finished?' asked her mum. 'Now I think it would be nice if George was to write on the card as well.'

Now George was only two, and so Rachel was a bit puzzled by this. 'How can George write on the card?' she asked. 'He can't write yet.'

'Well,' said Mum, 'you can help him. Just hold the card and put the pencil in his hand, and talk to him about what he is doing. Sit him on your lap.'

Rachel went into the living room, where George was sitting on the floor playing with his Thomas the Tank Engine. He smiled when he saw Rachel, as he always did, said her name and held up his arms to be picked up.

'Come on, Georgie,' said Rachel. 'You're going to write a card for Dad, in the kitchen.'

'In the kitchen,' repeated George and pointed to the door.

She went into the kitchen, carrying George on her hip, and sat down at the table with him on her lap. She showed him the card, which he immediately wanted to pick up. Rachel fended him off and George protested a bit. Then Rachel put the pencil in George's hand and held his hand towards the card. George knew about making marks with a pencil, because he liked to draw and scribble on paper with his pencils and crayons.

George held the pencil in his fist and reached eagerly towards the card. Rachel was a bit worried that he might tear it, so she held it down on the table and got ready to grab George's hand if he started to get too excited. But she needn't have worried. George put the pencil on the card and made some energetic up and down movements with it, all over the poem in the middle and all over Rachel's own writing.

Before George did his writing, she thought she might be annoyed if he went over the top of what she had written, but she found she wasn't annoyed at all. She could still read her writing, and the poem in the middle of the page, and George's marks looked quite interesting spread all across the page.

'Good boy, George,' she said, 'You've written nicely on Dad's card. Then she persuaded George to give her the pencil and where she had written, 'From Rachel' she added, 'and George.'

George signs a card

'Look Mum!' she called. 'Georgie's written in the card. But it's not really writing, is it?'

Her mum said, 'Making marks on paper is the start of writing. Soon he'll start to do lines and circles that show he knows what he is aiming for.'

Rachel thought for a bit. 'It's an amazing thing, writing. It's marks on paper, like George's marks, and yet if you make the right shapes they mean things. One set of marks doesn't mean anything, and another set of marks means lots of things. You just have to learn how to make the right shapes.'

Mum took the card, and the next morning, before their dad went to work, Rachel and George watched him open all of his cards.

'Always leave the best till last,' he said, as he opened the card from Rachel and George. He looked first at the jokey picture on the front, and then he opened it and straightaway he saw that this year there was some of George's writing. 'What a lovely surprise!' he said.

Rachel went over and gave him a big hug. When George saw that, he went over too and climbed up on his dad's knee.

'Presents tonight, when we have our tea,' said mum. Dad cuddled Rachel and George. 'This is the best present,' he said. 'There won't be anything better than this.'

✦ Conclusion

Was baby George writing? What do you think?

He wanted to make a mark on the paper, and he knew that there was something special about it. He knew it was something to do with his dad, and he knew that Rachel wanted him to do it. For him it was writing.

Later on he will learn shapes that people will be able to read, and they will have meaning for them. All writing starts with marks on the paper. Later, it develops a shape and meaning. Some people get there quicker than others, but all of us get there in the end.

A prayer

Dear God, we thank you for the gift of writing. As we learn to write, we ask for your help through difficulties and frustrations. Give us courage and patience, and bless our teachers as they help us. Amen.

A thought

Writing is hard to learn. It is important to do it, because through writing you can bring happiness to other people.

Song suggestions

'Praise to God for things we see', *Someone's Singing Lord*, 20

'To build a memory', *Primary Assembly Song Book*, 49

Optional follow up

Children with access to under threes can collect examples of art and 'writing', and make a collage or wall display with labels and pictures of the children.

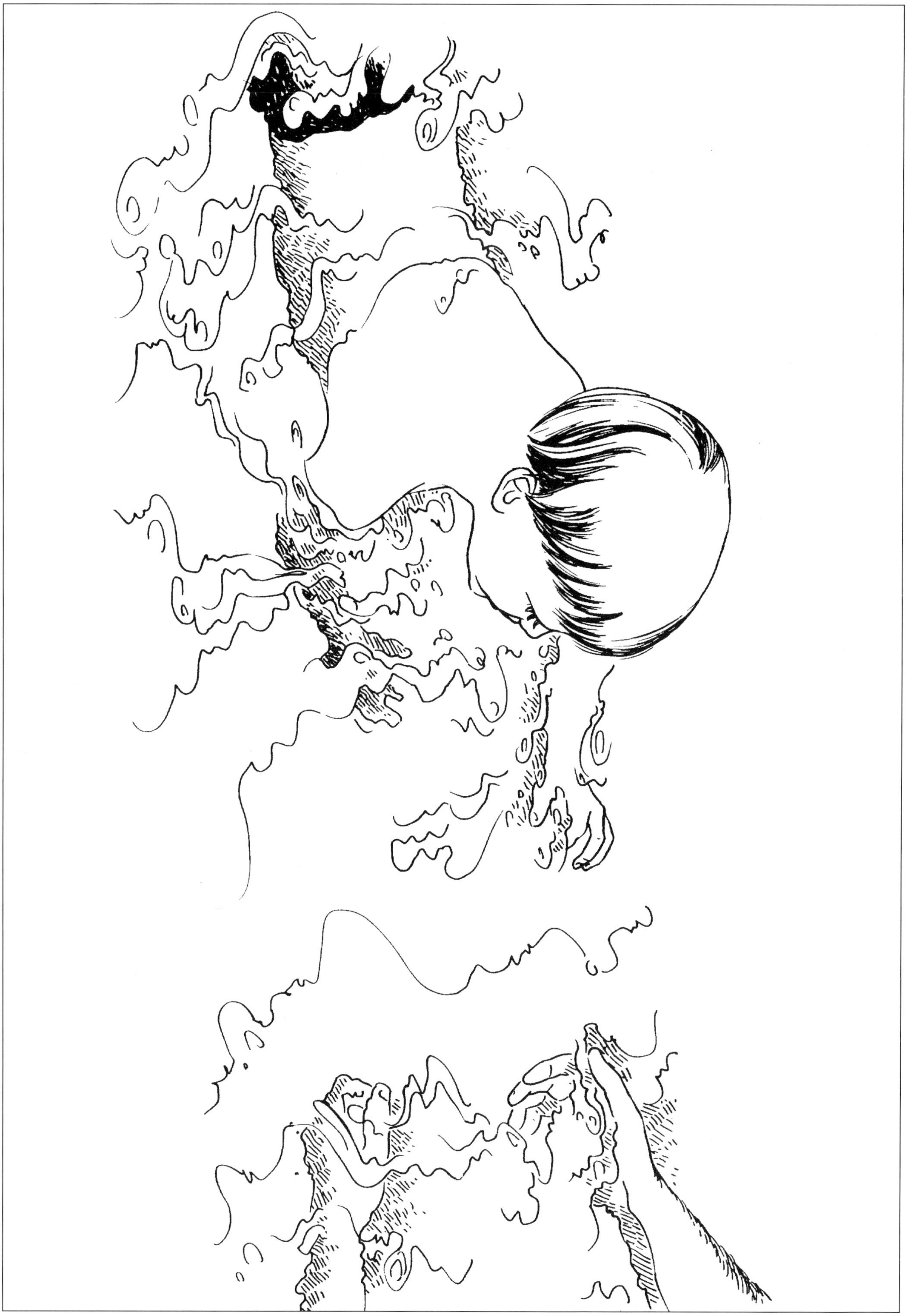

First swimming certificate

Assembly 3 of 4

This assembly is about keeping cheerful and confident when things are difficult. It tells of a child winning his first five-metre swimming certificate after trying for a long time.

You will need

- the OHT provided.

Taken by ....

Date ....

Given to ....

Comments

- ....
- ....
- ....

✦ Introduction

Our assembly today tells how a little boy achieved something after a great deal of effort and hard work.

So many of the things we do in life are difficult at the beginning. If you watch a baby of about nine or ten months, she really wants to talk – she makes all kinds of noises, and she can understand a lot of what you say, but she can't quite get the words out. And yet within a few months she's saying more words every day, and it's not really so difficult any more. It's often like that. There are things we want to do, but we have trouble getting started. For an adult, it might be driving lessons – once you've had the first lesson everything seems just a bit easier. But taking that first step is the most difficult thing.

When you learn to swim, the most difficult bit is the first time you get your feet off the bottom and actually swim, just for a few strokes. After that all you have to do is swim a little further each time. Somehow it seems easier after that first time. So many things we do are like that. Here's a story about a girl and her first swimming certificate.

🕮 Story

It was a special Friday assembly and Mrs Johnson had lots of certificates to give out. As the children came into the hall Mrs Johnson was still sorting out the certificates on the table at the front. She had her half-moon glasses on the end of her nose so that she could see clearly, and she was bending over the table.

The children all filed in and sat down, and Mrs Johnson carried on sorting out the certificates for a few moments, concentrating hard on what she was doing. Then she turned her head and looked up over the top of her glasses at the children. She pretended to be surprised to see them.

'Oh!' she said. 'You've all sneaked in while my back was turned. You were so quiet and good coming in that I didn't hear you!'

A little ripple of laughter ran through the hall, while Mrs Johnson walked to the front of her table and sat down on a chair looking at the

First swimming certificate

children. 'Good morning!' she said, and all the children said, 'Good morning Mrs Johnson. Good morning everybody!'

'Right!' said Mrs Johnson. 'Let's get on. We've got lots to do. First the song.'

Mrs Radcliffe played the piano, and everybody sang 'One More Step'. Then Mrs Johnson said a prayer, and all the children said 'Amen'.

'Now then!' said Mrs Johnson, and everyone sat up and looked at her. 'I have some swimming certificates to give out today. There are some for twenty-five metres, some for fifty metres, and one, would you believe this, for two hundred metres!'

Everyone went 'Oooh' at that, and Mrs Johnson opened her eyes wide and said again, 'Two hundred metres! That's an awfully long way. It's as far as from here to the Spar shop on the main road. It's as far as from here to the end of the senior school field. My word! I'd have trouble walking that far, let alone swimming it!'

Everybody laughed. Then Mrs Johnson said. 'Now, I wonder who won the two hundred-metre certificate?'

Actually, everybody knew. There was only one swimmer in the whole school who could possibly have done that – Mary Spurling. So everyone said, all together, 'Mary Spurling!' and Mrs Johnson said, 'Yes, that's right. So let's give her this special certificate.'

Everybody liked Mary. She was good at lots of things, and she went to a swimming club with her dad, so she was good at swimming. She came to the front and smiled at Mrs Johnson, and sat down holding her certificate, and her friends on each side leaned over to have a look at it.

'Now!' said Mrs Johnson, and everyone sat up again. 'Let's do the others. These are the people who have won fifty-metre certificates.' She read out the names, and they came to the front and shook hands with Mrs Johnson and sat down with their certificates.

'Now!' said Mrs Johnson, and everyone sat up again. 'These are the people who have won twenty-five-metre certificates.'

At the back of the hall, Michael Sullivan sat with his head down. He had some disappointed thoughts in his head. 'She's forgotten me,' thought Michael. 'I'm not going to get my certificate. I won't be able to go out there like Mary did, and get a certificate. Still, it wasn't much of one really.'

Michael thought about when he had won his certificate. It was at swimming only the day before. He had been at the baths with Mr Edwards, the teacher at the baths, who had said, 'Michael, you will get your feet off the bottom and swim five metres. I promise you.'

Michael had smiled a bit. He didn't really think that he would be able to do it. He really found it difficult in the water. At first he hadn't wanted to go in at all, but Mr Edwards had been really patient. He even went and got changed one day and went in the water with Michael and showed him that he could walk on the bottom and keep his head above the water. Then he showed Michael how he could put his face in the water and blow bubbles, and they laughed together.

As the weeks went by, Mr Edwards gave Michael lots of encouragement. He showed him how to hold on to the edge of the pool and dip his shoulders under. Then he showed him how he could hold on and let his feet come up off the bottom. All the time he kept praising Michael and telling him how well he was doing. He spent a lot of time with him, and let other teachers work with the other children further down the pool. Sometimes Michael got discouraged and thought he would never do it, but Mr Edwards wouldn't let him think like that. 'I know you can do it,' he said.

Then, only yesterday, Mr Edwards had leaned over the edge of the pool and told Michael to walk backwards towards the middle. When he had walked for a short distance he told him to stop. 'Now Michael,' he said. 'Swim to the edge of the pool. You can do this. Push off with your legs from the bottom, keep your head up and swim. Do it now!'

Put up the OHT provided.

And that's what he did. With his heart thumping, and gasping for breath, and making a lot of splash, Michael struck out for the edge of the pool. Mr Edwards encouraged him all the way. 'Keep going, Michael! Keep kicking. Now reach for the edge. Well done! Well done! Good boy!'

Michael reached the edge, then lowered his feet down, and stood there breathing heavily with a big smile, while Mr Edwards praised him. 'Now,' he said. 'I must write it down. Michael Sullivan. Five-metre certificate. Mustn't forget to give this to your teacher.'

And now Michael was sitting in assembly, wondering whether Mr Edwards had forgotten after all. He was starting to feel very disappointed, and a little tear was forming in the corner of his eye.

Then Mrs Johnson said. 'Now. That's all the swimming certificates done – except for one.'

At this, Michael started to cheer up. Mrs Johnson went on.

'To me,' she said, 'the most important swimming certificate is the very first one – the five-metre certificate. I think it's the most important because it can be the most difficult one to get and yet it's the start – after that the others come one after the other. Now come out here Michael Sullivan!'

Michael blushed and got to his feet and went out to the front. 'Now,' said Mrs Johnson. 'Michael only joined us this term. It's quite difficult to change school and start off in a new town, and I've watched him trying hard to make friends and do his work. And I've watched him also work really hard for this certificate, much harder than he will have to work for any of the others, I think. He never gave up. He was sure that one day he would be able to swim and he kept trying. Let's all give him a clap.'

And that's what everybody did.

But Mrs Johnson hadn't finished.

'For this special certificate,' she said, 'I've got somebody special to present it. Somebody who was just as determined as Michael to see him succeed. Come in Mr Edwards.'

Michael was really surprised when Mr Edwards came into the hall with a big smile on his face. He took the certificate from Mrs Johnson, shook Michael's hand and gave him a big smile. 'Well done, Michael!' he said.

Michael smiled and said thank you and thought how good it would be to take his certificate home for his dad to see. He had been really pleased when everyone clapped. He felt very pleased inside – really part of the school at last.

First swimming certificate

✦ Conclusion

What do you think? Do you think that Michael's five-metre certificate was more important than a fifty-metre or a two hundred-metre certificate? It's not easy to say, is it, because all the swimming certificates are important, and anyone who wins one deserves a good clap and a 'well done'. Mrs Johnson, though, thinks that the first one is especially important – once you have the first one, you can then carry on. Michael had to overcome his doubts and fears, and keep going when he could have given up. He was lucky to have a good swimming teacher, too.

Getting started can be the most difficult bit of anything new. It's not just swimming. It can be reading perhaps – you think you're never going to make a start, and you have to keep up your spirits and keep trying. Then one day it starts to happen and you make progress.

A prayer

Why don't you think of something that you are learning that seems difficult at the moment – swimming, reading, writing, tables? Then I'll say a prayer.

Lord, we ask for your help with the thing we find difficult. Help us to stay cheerful. Help us to get started. And thank you for the people who work with us and stick with us until we have success. Amen.

A thought

Michael kept going with his swimming until he heard the words 'Well done!' That's a good thing to aim for in whatever we are doing.

Song suggestions

'I did it!', *Primary Assembly Song Book, 87*

'For all the strength we have', *Someone's Singing Lord*, 16

Optional follow up

Try to remember things that you can do easily now, but which seemed very difficult at first. Can you remember the feeling when you first succeeded?

I can do it

Assembly 4 of 4

This assembly is about a child who is helped by his uncle through a bad patch in his learning. The message is of reassurance – that everyone hits difficult patches in life and learning, and that it's almost always possible to get through them and go on to success.

You will need

- ***Optional*** blank OHT and a packet of table salt.

Taken by ....

Date ....

Given to ....

Comments

- ....
- ....
- ....

✦ Introduction

Our assembly today is going to show us that we can often do better than we thought we could – we need some encouragement, some confidence, and some good examples to look up to.

In this assembly, Benjie's uncle shows him a new way to approach his problem with writing and helps him to have the confidence to keep trying and to achieve success.

Today I want us to think about getting stuck.

I wonder how many of you have ever put your hand up in class and said, 'Please, Miss, I'm stuck'.

I wonder what that means?

Does it mean you've sat on some glue and you can't get up from your chair?

Well it might mean that, but that's not what we're talking about here is it?

I think it means when you come to something that you're doing and you can't get past it. Perhaps it's a word that you can't read. You're going along, reading away, and then suddenly there's this difficult word waiting to trip you up. You're buzzing along, and you come to a sudden stop.

So what do you do? You look at it for a bit, then you try the things we've taught you about breaking the word down, but you still can't get it. And so you decide that you're stuck, and you put up your hand, and the teacher says, 'Yes, what is it?' and you say, 'Miss, I'm stuck!'

What happens next? Teacher comes across when she has a minute, and she sits or kneels down beside you and helps you. She might just tell you the word, but what she'll probably do is help you to read it for yourself. You'll spend a bit of time on it, and then suddenly you're not stuck any more. You're unstuck in fact, and off you go again.

Now that's not so bad. You get stuck, somebody helps you, and off you go again.

Sometimes, though, you can get stuck a bit more seriously than that. Sometimes there's something that you just can't understand no matter how hard you try. You go home

I can do it

thinking, 'I'll never get that. I'll never be able to do that.' It can make you quite unhappy if it goes on for too long.

The first thing to say is that everyone, me, your teachers, all the other children, have had an experience like that. We still do sometimes. We all have problems that seem too big to be solved – but we usually sort them out in the end.

So, if you do get stuck, try not to get too upset. There are 'getting stuck' moments all through our lives. Sometimes we need a bit of patience and a bit of help. And in the end we may do better than we ever thought.

That's what happened to Benjie in this story.

Story

Sometimes, everything feels sunny and warm, even if the weather isn't very sunny and warm. Sometimes, you have a good feeling inside because everything's going well.

And sometimes, it's the opposite. Everything feels dark and rainy, even if the weather isn't dark and rainy. Sometimes, you have a bad, lumpy feeling inside because nothing's going well at all.

Well, Benjie was having these bad, lumpy feelings. When his Aunt Kate met him at the school gate his mouth would be turned down at the corners, and his shoulders would be hunched up.

And when she said to him, 'What did you do at school today, Benjie?' he would just grunt something and turn his face away.

At home, when he was having his tea with Aunt Kate and Uncle Matthew, he would just sit there, not eating very much and looking very grumpy. And sometimes he would cry for no reason.

Aunt Kate and Uncle Matthew were very worried about him. Benjie was usually a very happy boy, full of life, and ready for anything – a big bundle of fun. But he wasn't a bundle of fun now. He was a bag of misery.

In the end, it was Uncle Matthew who got the story out of him.

'I'm stuck, Uncle Mattie,' said Benjie, with tears in his eyes.

'Well,' said his uncle, 'that's no surprise to me. I guessed it was something like that. Now, what are you stuck on?'

'I'm never going to be able to write,' said Benjie, and great big round tears came rolling down his cheeks.

'Oh, I don't believe that,' said Uncle Matthew. 'It may be hard now, but you'll get the trick of it, sure enough.'

'I never will,' wailed Benjie. 'All the other children can write. They write all the time in their books and on paper, and I can't do it. I can't make my hand do what I want it to. I can read, but I can't make my hand do the writing.'

'Well,' said Uncle Matthew. 'Let me tell you a big secret. When I was a little boy, I surely couldn't write either. Mind you, I couldn't read till I was eight, because I didn't go to school much. And even then it was my old grannie who taught me. And she taught me to write too. She taught me in the sand on the beach outside her little wooden house.'

I can do it

'In the sand?' said Benjie. His eyes had dried up and he was suddenly very interested.

'In the sand, yes,' said Uncle Matthew. He was quiet for a moment. In his mind was the memory of the warm sun, and the beach with children playing in the water. And his grannie's house, filled with love and laughter. So long ago, but so clear in his mind.

Uncle Matthew sighed, and Benjie waited patiently for him to go on.

Then Uncle Matthew said, 'She would smooth a big patch of sand with her hands and she would take a stick and she would write letters in the sand. And I would take another stick and I would write those letters too. And I learned to write just like that. From my old grannie, God bless her.'

'I wish we had some sand,' said Benjie. 'You could teach me to write in the sand.'

'Well, I tell you what we do have.' Matthew went to the pantry cupboard and brought out a big packet.

He said, 'I have here a big packet of salt. I'm going to clear all the things off the kitchen table like this. Then I'm going to pour all this lovely white salt on the kitchen table … like this. Then I'm going to smooth it out just like my grannie would smooth out the sand. Then I'm going to get my finger and I'm going to write "Benjie" in the salt with my finger. Like this.'

Optional

At this point, do the same with your packet of salt and the blank OHT. Carefully pour the salt, so as not to get it anywhere it shouldn't go. Switch on the projector, and write in the salt with your finger.

Benjie watched, absolutely thrilled by what he was seeing. He'd never thought that you could write on the kitchen table in salt. It was a new idea. Perhaps he would be able to do that.

'Now you write "Benjie" too,' said Uncle Matthew. And that's what Benjie did. He got it a bit wrong at first, because it's quite a complicated name to write when you think about it. But it was easy for Uncle Matthew to rub it out and let him have another try, and Benjie didn't mind that.

So, each day, Benjie had a salty writing lesson on the kitchen table with his Uncle Matthew. They would write words and names together, and Uncle Matthew would tell stories about his childhood in the village of Laborie in St Lucia.

It helped Benjie a lot. Of course he was really learning most of his writing at school, but just doing something a bit different with Uncle Matthew, and having Uncle Matthew being interested in him and telling him stories helped him a lot. And sure enough, he soon unstuck himself and started to make real progress.

Then came the day when he wrote a story for his teacher that started, 'This is how my Uncle Matthew learned to write in the sand. And this is how Uncle Matthew taught me to write in the salt.'

His teacher thought the story was beautiful, and he had to take it to the headteacher for a gold star, and the headteacher put Benjie's story on the wall of her room. 'I'd like to meet your Uncle Matthew one day,' she said.

I can do it

✦ Conclusion

Do you think that Uncle Matthew taught Benjie to write? Well, I don't think he did it all. Benjie was learning at school how to write. But what his Uncle Mattie did was help Benjie to get himself unstuck. He gave him something a bit different to do, and took an interest in him, and Benjie gained a bit of confidence. Benjie started to say to himself, 'Maybe I can do this after all.'

Have you ever written in the sand with a stick? Try a lolly stick if you can't find anything else. If there's enough sand – such as on a beach – you can write really big, much bigger than you can on paper, or in books.

Always remember – anyone can get stuck. What you need to get unstuck is a bit of help, a bit of time and a lot of confidence. Then, once you're unstuck, you'll make real progress.

A prayer

Lord, help us when our work gets too hard. Help us to stay calm and thoughtful, and to accept the advice of other people. Give us confidence and help us to stay cheerful. Amen.

A thought

When a tractor gets stuck in the mud, the driver has to stay calm and do all the things he's been taught to do. He needs a bit of outside help, too. And when the tractor comes unstuck, it shoots forward, faster than before.

Song suggestions

'The journey of life', *Someone's Singing Lord*, 28

'I did it!', *Primary Assembly Song Book*, 87

What's the difference?

Assembly 1 of 4

This is an infant level assembly. It celebrates the differences between people and helps children to see that while some things about them will change as they grow up, others will remain the same all their lives.

You will need

- the OHT provided.

Taken by ....

Date ....

Given to ....

Comments

- ....
- ....
- ....

Story

Alisha was fed up and told her mum.

'Why are you fed up, Alisha?' asked her mum.

'I'm not sure really. I'm just feeling fed up,' Alisha replied.

'Have you fallen out with your friends again, Alisha?' asked her mum.

'Well, in a way,' Alisha admitted.

'What have you fallen out about this time, Alisha?' asked her mum.

'They keep getting on at me about my hair,' said Alisha.

'I think your hair's really nice. We spend ages on it every night and every morning,' her mum replied.

'Well, Kate says my hair's not as nice as hers. She's got really long blonde hair,' said Alisha.

'Well, Alisha, come on now. Your hair is just like mine. It's lovely and dark, and we spend ages braiding it,' said her mum.

'I want it to be blonde, like Kate's. Can I have it dyed blonde?' said Alisha.

'When you're old enough to make your own mind up, you can dye it any colour you want. Until then, it stays like it is. I'm proud of my hair, and my skin, and my clothes, and you should be too,' said her mum.

But Alisha was still moody when she went to bed, and moody again when she went to school next day.

At school, she sat behind Kate in assembly. She played with Kate's hair while Mrs Johnson was talking. Mrs Johnson frowned at her once or twice and she stopped doing it. Kate's hair was shiny in the sun, and Alisha thought it looked really nice.

Back at home, Alisha's mum was having a good think about Alisha. When Alisha's mum had been at school, all the children had more or less the same kind of hair and hairstyle and nobody took any notice. Now, though, there were so many different kinds, and Alisha was quite sensitive about it.

Alisha's mum thought that Alisha was really beautiful. She was quite tall for her age, and she had a lovely smile. Why, she looked just like one of those models that advertised cars!

What's the difference?

What nonsense to think that she ought to have blonde hair.

She sat down and had a cup of tea, and looked at the mantelpiece where Alisha's birthday cards were on display. She smiled to herself. The birthday card from Kate had a little blonde girl on it. Trust Kate to send that. She was a smashing little girl and a good friend for Alisha but she really ought not to go on about her hair like she did.

Then Alisha's mum had a brainwave. She went and rummaged in her toolbox for a craft knife, and then went looking around for a photograph of Alisha. There were plenty to choose from.

When Alisha came home from school, her mum was in the kitchen singing to herself. 'Hello, Alisha. Everything OK?' Alisha just grunted. She was still sulking a bit. 'Still sulking about that hair of yours?' her mum asked. 'Never mind, I've managed to change it for you.'

'What do you mean, Mum?' Alisha asked.

'New hair, Alisha. That's what! Just look!' said her mum, pointing to the sideboard. There, in a frame, was a photograph of Alisha – one of her school photographs. It was a good picture – she was smiling, and her eyes had those little points of light in them that good photographers can manage to catch. But her hair! It was all blonde!

Alisha's mum had carefully cut out the blonde curly hair from the little girl on Kate's birthday card, and fitted it to Alisha on her school photograph. It fitted exactly, and you couldn't see the join unless you looked really closely.

Alisha dropped her bag and picked up the photograph and then sat down on the settee. She stared at the photograph. She saw her own lovely brown face surrounded by a mass of blonde curls. She stared and stared. Then she looked up at her mum.

'Mum! It looks *really awful*!' she said.

Alisha's mum behaved very casually.

'It does, doesn't it? Dreadful, isn't it? Terrible, isn't it?' said her mum.

'Can you take it off? Is my own hair still underneath?' asked Alisha anxiously.

'Oh yes. It'll come off alright. Give it here a minute,' said her mum.

In no time, Alisha's photograph was back to normal. Alisha sat thinking for a while. Then she said, 'Kate's hair looks really nice. But it looks nice on Kate.'

'That's right!' said her mum. 'Kate's hair looks good on Kate. Steve's hair looks good on Steve. Pritpal's hair looks good on Pritpal. Alisha's hair looks good on Alisha. Right?'

'Right! When I see Kate's mum I'm going to ask her to do the same for one of Kate's photographs,' said Alisha.

'Good idea. But I bet she won't find a birthday card with a little girl like you on it!' said her mum. And they both laughed.

✦ Activity

(Put up the OHT) 'This is Alisha's group. Let's read the names – Lucy, Kate, Leon, Manjit, David, Gary, Nula, Craig, Alisha, Pritpal.'

Let's think of some of the differences between them. Can we write any of them down under the picture?

(Examples might include: Gary wears glasses, Kate uses a wheelchair...)

They are all different, aren't they. And yet they are all members of the class and of the school. Just as you are all different and yet you are all equal members of the school.

It's good to admire our friends and to like their clothes and their hair. But it's good to remember that what is good about them may not suit you. Be comfortable with yourself. Your friends like you for what you are. We like you for what you are.

Here's a poem by Gerald Haigh about everybody being different, and about growing bigger day by day.

Fat, thin, high, low
Short, tall, fast, slow
Sorry, scatty, silly, soppy
Merry, happy, jolly, spotty
Black, yellow, brown, white
Sleepy, lively, dim, bright

Look around us and you'll see
We're all different – you from me
Him from her, girl from boy
John from Sandeep, Jane from Roy

An adult's big and fully grown
A baby can't be left alone
Children at school are in between
Growing fast 'till we're eighteen

Last year's shoes are much too tight
I'm taller than I was last night
Now I'm looking down on Lee
Next year he'll look down on me!

✦ Optional activity

Bring a group of volunteers to the front – as many as you feel comfortable about handling, say up to twelve.

Look at all these lovely people. (We think they are all lovely anyway!) They're all lovely but different. They have different faces, different hair, different clothes. They're different sizes as well. And yet they all belong to our school. They are all equal and all loved by us and by God.

We can't exchange their hair, in the way that Alisha's mum exchanged it in the photograph. Let's try exchanging some of our clothes.

Use some sensitivity here, but have a general exchange of jackets, tops, shoes. Have some fun. Join in. Perhaps other adults will join in.

As a settler down – repeat the poem, with the pupils joining in.

Whoever we are, God loves us.
We are all equal in his sight.
Nobody is better than anybody else.
Every one of us is beautiful.

A prayer

Dear God, you made us. We rejoice that we are all different. If we were all the same, how would we know each other? Help us to love our friends without being jealous of them. Help us to be comfortable with ourselves. Amen.

A thought

Differences are important. Our differences make us what we are. We know each other because we are different from each other.

Song suggestions

'I would like to be', *Tinder Box*, 45
'The ink is black, the page is white', *Someone's Singing Lord*, 39

What's the difference?

I'm much bigger inside

Assembly 2 of 4

This assembly is about the difference between physical size and the size of personality. It takes the example of a child who is small for his age.

You will need

- nothing at all.

Taken by ....

Date ....

Given to ....

Comments

- ....
- ....
- ....

✦ Introduction

This assembly looks at different meanings of measurement when talking about a person. If we say someone is a 'big person' it can have different meanings.

Call to the front everybody of a particular age, for example all the six year olds or four year olds.

Now, what is the thing that is the same about all these children? Yes they are all the same age.

But are they the same in any other ways?

It's not easy to find other ways in which they are the same, is it?

Are they all boys or all girls? No.

Do they all have the same kind of hair or the same colour eyes? No.

Are they all the same size? No.

They are all different. Some are tall, some are shorter. Yet they are all the same age.

It's good that they are all different. It wouldn't do for everyone to be the same. So before these people sit down, let's say a prayer of thanks for our differences.

Lord, we thank you for the differences between us. We thank you for tall people and short people, for people with blue eyes and brown eyes and green eyes, for people with light hair and dark hair and red hair and no hair. For people with brown skins and black skins and pink skins. For people who walk and people who travel in wheelchairs. These differences are what make us interesting. Help us to live together in friendship and always to enjoy our differences.

Ask the volunteers to sit down.

Has anyone ever been worried by being different from some other people? You can be honest, because we've all had that feeling. This story is about James, who was bothered about being small for his age.

 ISBN 1 874050 55 4 pfp, 61 Gray's Inn Road, London WC1X 8TH

I'm much bigger inside

Story

James was sometimes known as the pocket rocket or the flying metre. That was because he was quite small for his age – just one metre tall – and yet he was very active and always running about and getting into things.

'James is quite small, but he's all there!' was something that his aunt was always saying.

Most of the time he didn't mind, but one evening when he was in Year 2, it really got to him.

'What's up with you James?' said his mum.

'I'm fed up with people calling me Titch!' said James. 'The other kids just keep on about it.'

'They shouldn't do that,' said his mum. 'Anyway, I bet they don't know who Little Titch really was. He was a famous music hall act – a very small man who did singing and dancing on the stage.'

James wasn't really comforted by that.

'They all say things, even the teachers. They call me "Little James" instead of just "James" and I don't like it.'

'Well let me tell you something,' said his mum. 'The same thing happens to your dad. He's smaller than usual for a grown-up man, and although people don't mean to be cruel, they do make jokes about his size and call him "Little Alf". He can get upset about it, but he soon gets over it.'

That night, James was lying awake when he heard his dad come in from work.

His dad usually came in quite late, but he always popped up to see him. Sure enough the door of his room opened and his dad came in and sat down on the edge of the bed.

His dad put a hand on James's head and stroked his hair.

'Your mum says you've been a bit upset,' said his dad. 'About being small.'

James sniffed a bit, but didn't speak.

'Well I'll tell you about when I was about your age,' said his dad. 'I was small, too. One day when I got upset, your gran – my mum, the gran you don't remember – told me that it's how big you are inside that counts, not how big you are outside.'

James kept on listening.

His dad carried on, 'She said I was brave and energetic, kind and very funny. And you know, James, that's you too. You are one metre tall on the outside, but inside, well let's see. You are kind to your mum – that's one metre. You make us laugh, so that's another metre. You work hard at your school lessons, so that's another metre. So inside you are three metres. And we love you another three metres, so you are six metres tall. Much taller and you would be Godzilla.'

James laughed as his dad tucked him in.

When his dad had gone, James drifted off to sleep. As he slept, he had a special dream that went like this.

A big Alsatian dog met a little terrier in the farmyard one day.

'I'm a better dog than you,' said the big Alsatian. 'I'm big and strong.'

I'm much bigger inside

'I'm a better dog than you,' said the terrier, 'I'm small, cute and cuddly.'

A wise old horse was looking over the door of its stable and heard the two dogs. 'You silly dogs,' he said. 'Remember this – not better, not worse, just different!'

✦ Conclusion

It's what you are inside that counts. Being small, tall or different from others in some other way can make you self-conscious. It's worse if people point it out to you or make fun. But what really matters is what you are like inside. In the end, that is what people notice.

Jesus had strong words to say to people who made quick judgments about others. He looked for the best qualities in others, and we can learn from that example.

A prayer

Lord, we thank you for living creatures of all kinds, sizes and colours. We thank you for the differences between them. We thank you for the differences between human beings. Help us to judge people by their actions and not by how they look. Amen.

A thought

It's what's inside a book that counts, not whether it's a big book, a small one or one with a pretty cover.

Song suggestions

'Sing a song of people', *Tinder Box*, 18

'Same but different', *Primary Assembly Song Book*

Optional follow up

If there are, for example, wheelchair users in class, or pupils who are known to be sensitive about their body shapes, it may be enough to leave the assembly to stand on its own. You might just discuss the advantages of different sizes and body shapes – jockeys, rugby players and basketball players. (RE/PSE)

Are we bullies then?

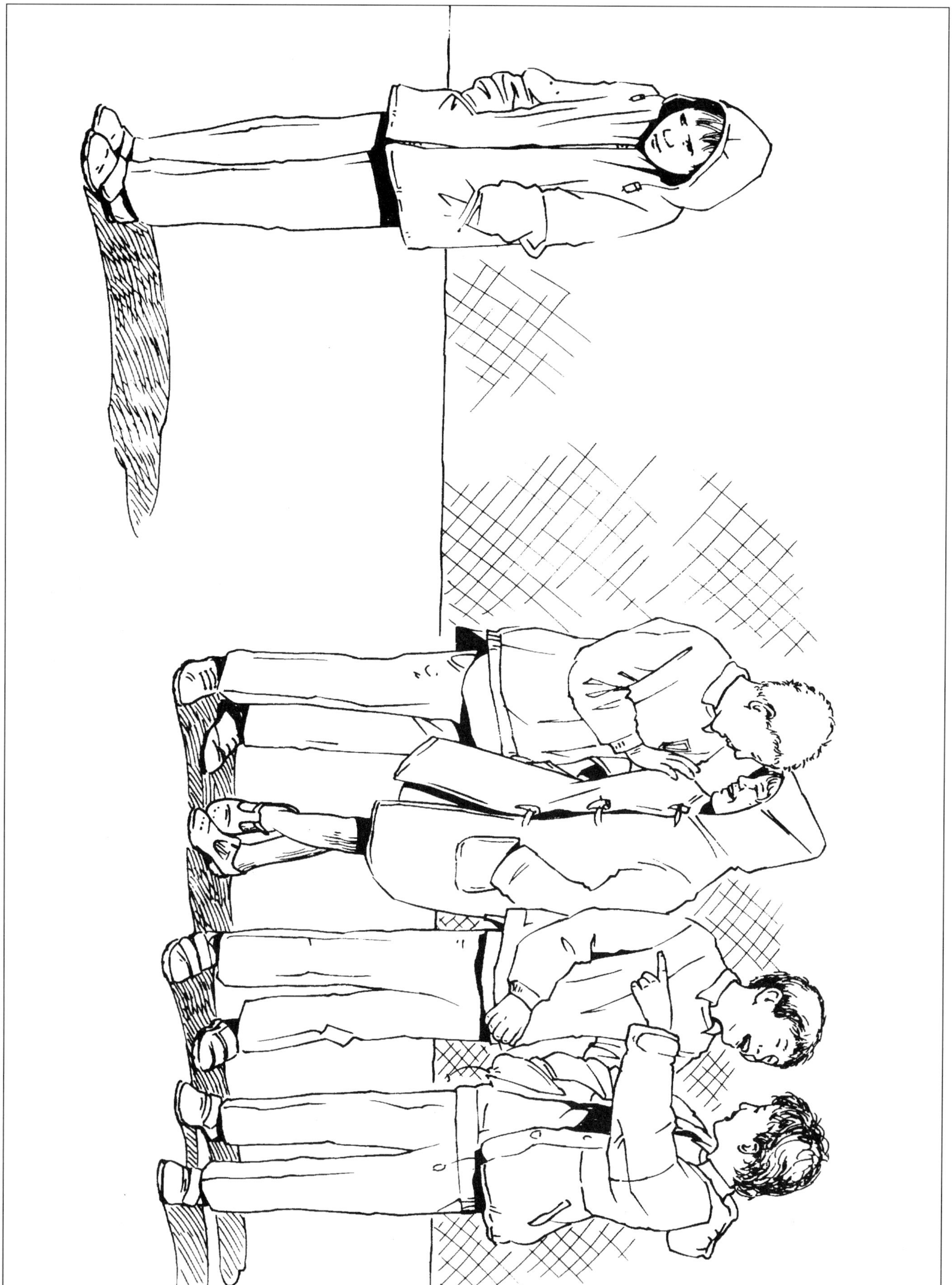

Are we bullies then?

Assembly 3 of 4

This assembly is about bullying. It approaches bullying, however, from the point of view of the bullies, and it shows that some members of a bullying group may be unwilling, and may even be unaware of the reality of what they are doing.

You will need

- the OHT supplied.

Taken by ....

Date ....

Given to ....

Comments

- ....
- ....
- ....

✦ Introduction

In this assembly we see how a little boy tries to make friends. He finds, however, that some friends try to lead him into being a bully. When that happens he has to make a brave decision.

Be honest now, have you ever been unkind to anyone? I think the answer is yes, because if we're honest, every one of us has been unkind to somebody at one time or another. It's just one of those things about human beings. We might call somebody a cruel name, push or hit someone, or snatch something that we want from someone else.

When we do any of these things we know it's wrong. Afterwards we wish we hadn't done it, and we say we won't do it again.

But sometimes we are unkind in a thoughtless way. Not because we do something, but because we don't do something. We might fail to see that a friend is unhappy or do nothing to help someone who is being badly treated by other children.

Most of the time we aren't unkind. Most of the time we help each other. Most of the time we comfort each other when we have problems.

Sometimes, though, we do act in thoughtless ways. In Gordon's class, one day, there was some real thoughtlessness that made one person very unhappy until it was sorted out.

🕮 Story

As Gordon settled down in his class, he made three special friends – Gemma, Robert and Carlos. He talked about them a lot at home. 'Gemma likes football,' he'd say, or 'Carlos knows some good jokes,' and Gordon's mum would smile and say, 'You'll have to ask them to come round to play at our house one day.'

Gordon would ask them that at school. 'Will you come round to our house?' he would say, but they never seemed to want to do that.

Put up the OHT provided.

Then, one day, Gordon said something that worried his mum a little. He was sitting on the

Are we bullies then?

floor playing with a model train and he said, without looking up, 'We don't like Mark.'

'Pardon,' said Gordon's mum. 'Who don't you like?'

'We don't like Mark,' said Gordon again. 'Me and Gemma and Robert and Carlos don't like Mark.'

'Why don't you like him, Gordon?' asked his mum. 'Has he done anything to you?'

Gordon shrugged his shoulders. 'We don't like him,' he said again.

Gordon didn't say any more. His mum worried about what he had said. Gordon didn't sound happy when he said it and, come to think of it, she realised that he'd been a bit quiet lately, and not said much about his school friends.

So she decided to go and speak to Mrs Fulton, Gordon's teacher, to see if everything was going well in class.

'I'm glad you came,' said Mrs Fulton, 'because I am a bit worried. I think Mark is unhappy, and I think the reason he's unhappy is that Gordon and Gemma and Robert and Carlos are being unkind to him.'

Gordon's mum was shocked by this. 'You mean they are bullying him?' she said. 'You mean our Gordon is bullying somebody?'

'Perhaps,' said Mrs Fulton. 'I don't think Gordon sees it like that. I think he's just joining in with his friends. They call Mark names, and pretend that he smells and things like that. They don't hit him or anything, but they are certainly cruel in some ways. For some reason Robert doesn't like Mark, and the others are friends with Robert so they've decided that they don't like Mark either. I'm not sure they really enjoy what they are doing. I think that's why Gordon told you, because he wanted you to try to sort it out for him somehow. I'm trying to deal with it and I was going to send you a note this week.'

That evening, Gordon's mum had a word with Gordon.

'What's the problem with Mark then?' she asked. 'Are you being unkind to him?'

Gordon didn't say anything. 'We don't like him, I think,' he said.

Then he started to cry. Gordon's mum put her arms round him and sat him on her knee.

'You know, Gordon,' she said. 'I don't think that you should be unkind to anybody, and especially someone who isn't doing you any harm. We didn't teach you to be unkind to people. Look how carefully you treat our animals and your sister. You're a kind boy, not a cruel one.'

Gordon cried even more when she said that.

'Tell you what, Gordon,' she said. 'I think you should tell Robert that you don't want to be unkind to Mark any more, and I think you should try to be friends with Mark.'

'But Robert won't like me then,' sniffed Gordon.

'Well, I think that's up to him,' said his mum. 'If he wants to be friends with you he can. But you shouldn't do wrong things just because he wants you to. In your heart you know that don't you?'

Gordon nodded.

Next day, on the playground, Gordon went across to talk to Mark. 'Hello Mark,' he said. 'Can I play with you this morning?'

Mark looked surprised, but he said yes.

Are we bullies then?

A few minutes later Robert and Gemma came across. 'We don't want you to play with Mark,' said Robert. Gordon looked at him. 'Well, I want to play with Mark. Do you want to play with us?'

Robert walked away, but Gemma stayed. Like Gordon, she hadn't really wanted to be unkind to Mark, and when Gordon made friends with Mark it gave her the courage to do the same.

✦ Conclusion

Gordon had a problem. He wanted to be friends with Robert and the others. But Robert was doing something that Gordon didn't really like. Robert was being unkind to Mark – calling him names and pushing him. Gordon thought that he should join in doing this. He thought that Robert would not be friends with him if he didn't join in.

Gordon had to make up his mind what to do. Should he carry on being unkind to Mark, or should he refuse to do that, even if Robert fell out with him? Inside himself he really knew what the right thing was, and his mum helped him to see it. You see, you shouldn't be unkind to other people at all. And it's even worse if you're doing it just because somebody wants you to do it.

This is what I want you to think about – if somebody you think is a friend wants you to do something that you know is wrong, then that person is not really a good friend at all. Gordon discovered that, and his mum helped him to think it through. He did the right thing in the end.

When you find yourself being drawn into being unkind to someone else, it always helps to say, 'Would I like this if it happened to me?' Before you do something to someone else – call them a name, or say something unkind – just ask yourself that question, 'Would I like this if it happened to me?'

One of the things that Jesus teaches us is that we ought always to put ourselves in the place of the people we are dealing with. In the Lord's prayer, which Jesus taught us, we ask to be forgiven – 'just as we forgive the people who do wrong things to us.'

A prayer

Lord, help us when we have to make difficult choices in our lives. Give us the courage to do the right thing. Give us the wisdom to ask for help and advice. Amen.

A thought

We often have to choose which path to take. When we make the choice, we should try not to follow someone down the path that we know is wrong.

Song suggestions

'Friends', *Primary Assembly Song Book*, 83

'Think, think on these things', *Someone's Singing Lord*, 38

Optional follow up

It can be a good exercise just to sit and talk, and perhaps to write, about how we like to be treated by other people. The obvious extension – that we should therefore treat other people in that way – can either be left implicit or could form part of further discussion.

The Hare and the Tortoise

The Hare and the Tortoise

'I can run much faster than you,' said the hare,
'I'll run far and fast to who knows where.
My legs are so strong, my feet are so quick
I'll be out of your sight in just half a tick!'

'That may well be true,' the tortoise said,
As out of the shell he poked his head.
'But can you keep going, all day and all night?
Or will you get tired? I think you might.'

'You're just an old slowcoach,' the hare replied.
'To prove it we'll race down the road side by side.
You watch me, I'll leave you behind at the start.
At the end we'll be half of the county apart.'

'That may also be true,' the tortoise agreed.
For you certainly do have a greater top speed.
But a sprinter like you, when it comes to long distance,
Is likely to need a little assistance.'

'Assistance! Assistance!' the hare said in scorn.
'I need only the legs with which I was born.
My own rapid feet and my supercharged knees
Will ensure that I'll beat you with startling ease.'

'Well, let's wait and see,' said the tortoise that day.
'We'll both run this race to a place far away.
Line up here beside me and wait for the gun.
At the end of the story we'll see who has won!'

The Hare and the Tortoise

Assembly 4 of 4

This assembly is based on the fable of the Hare and the Tortoise, which sets out to show that slow and steady is better than quick and erratic. The assembly shows that there are different, but equally valid, ways of working.

You will need

- the OHT provided.

Taken by ....

Date ....

Given to ....

Comments

- ....
- ....
- ....

✦ Introduction

In our assembly today we'll see that there are different ways to achieve something and that the quickest way is not always the best. We must try to find the way which suits us best, which may not be the way others would choose.

Who can run fast? Lots of you can. Who can win races? Lots of you can. Are they both the same, do you think? Do you think that being able to run fast means that you will always win races?

Well, it's usually true, I suppose, but when you think about it, maybe it's not always like that. For one thing, a person who can sprint very fast for a short distance, may not be able to keep it up for very long. He may go very fast and then stop, all out of puff, unable to keep going to the end.

Or a person who can sprint very fast may not be able to concentrate on the race. She might see her mum and sister at the side of the track and go over to talk to them while everyone else goes on to the finish. Or she might start day-dreaming about a big and beautiful ice cream, and forget to run hard to the end.

There are lots of stories like that. For example, there's the one about a tortoise and a hare. Now the tortoise, as you know, is a very slow-moving animal. It carries its house on its back, so it has quite a weight to move around. How fast could you go if you had to carry your house around?

The hare, on the other hand, has no shell. And although it looks a lot like a rabbit, it doesn't live in a burrow. It has to spend all its time on the ground, in open fields. That means it has to be able to run faster than the animals that might want to catch it and eat it. So the hare is very fast and the tortoise is very slow. Each protects itself in its own way – the tortoise with its hard shell, the hare with its speed.

The legend goes that one day a tortoise and a hare had a race – a long race down a long and dusty road, on a very hot day. Here's a poem to set the scene for us.

Put up the OHT supplied and read out the poem.

The Hare and the Tortoise

Story

Harold Hare and Timolena Tortoise were having an argument. Harold Hare, as always, was boasting.

'I'm dead quick, me,' he said. 'I'm the fastest thing around. I can go faster than, ooh, faster than a very fast thing. Faster than a speeding carrot.'

'Huh,' said Timolena a bit stuffily. 'Speed is not everything. Flashy sprinting is not always the answer. Determined steady effort might do the trick you know. Going slowly but steadily might be better in the end.'

'No chance,' said Harold. 'I'm so quick, that even if I stopped for a drink and a turnip, I'd still be faster in the end.'

Timolena was not to be put off. She was a determined tortoise as, indeed, all tortoises are.

'What we need to do,' she said, 'is have a race. Down the Long Lane. You and me. Just the two of us. To see who wins.'

Harold Hare roared with laughter, 'Oh dearie me,' he said. 'A race? You and me? Slowcoach against the fast guy! What an idea! When? Where?'

'Tomorrow,' said Timolena. 'At the top of Long Lane. The grasshoppers will start us off.'

'See you tomorrow then,' said Harold Hare. 'Tee hee, chuckle chuckle. My word. Oh dear.'

The next day, the two racers stood side by side at the start of the Long Lane. The grasshoppers hopped and chirruped around, and the senior grasshoppers said, 'On your marks ! Get set! Go!'

Well! As you might expect, Harold Hare shot off like a speeding bullet, leaving all the grasshoppers coughing and chirruping in a cloud of dust. And Timolena started on her long and lonely plod.

After a few yards, Harold spun around. 'Ha ha!' he cried. 'Can't catch me, I'm the fast guy. Watch me goooooooooo!'

And off he sped into the dim distance, while Timolena still plodded on.

Soon, Harold Hare found himself racing along the white and dusty road all alone in the hot sun. He stopped.

'Ha ha!' he said. 'I am so far ahead I can stop for a turnip.' So off he went into the nearby field to find a turnip. He kept an eye on the road, and soon Timolena Tortoise came into view, plodding along. He ate his turnip, then, when Timolena was nearly up to him, he set off again.

Soon, once again, Harold Hare found himself racing along the white and dusty road all alone in the hot sun. He stopped again. 'Ha ha!' he said. 'I am so far ahead I can stop for a lettuce.' So off he went into the nearby field to find a lettuce. He kept an eye on the road, and soon Timolena Tortoise came into view, plodding along. 'There's still a long way to go,' he said to himself. 'So I'll have a little rest and I'll still be able to catch her up.'

It was a hot day, and the lettuce and the turnip had been so very nice. He rested, and he shut his eyes for a moment. And what do you think?

Yes, he fell asleep. And when he woke up, what do you think? Yes, it was much later than he wanted it to be. The sun was going down, the Long Lane was looking dark and lonely.

'Oh my!' he said to himself. 'Must be extra quick now.' And off he sped, faster and faster, kicking up great clouds of white dust on Long Lane. Soon the end of the Lane came into view. In the distance, he could see the grasshoppers holding a tape across the road. And, oh dear, he could see Timolena Tortoise, still plodding along, just about to go through the tape.

Harold Hare put in a desperate spurt. His legs became a blur. His long ears were flattened back by the wind. His feet pounded the dusty road. He nearly made it, but Timolena Tortoise crossed the line just half a second ahead of him.

Was he annoyed? He certainly was. 'You might have won,' he said, 'but I'm still faster than you.'

Timolena smiled a slow smile and blinked a slow blink, as tortoises do. 'Let's leave it at that, then,' she said. 'You're the fastest, but I'm the one who wins the races.'

That, of course, started another argument, and the two of them went off arguing – Harold getting so excited that he kept galloping ahead of Timolena and having to come back so he could talk to her. What a waste of effort! But that's another story I think.

✦ Conclusion

The Hare and the Tortoise is a traditional story that's always told because of what it can teach us. What does the story teach us, do you think? Let's listen in on Class 2 while they talk about it.

Sian says, 'Miss, I think it says that if you work hard and steadily, that's better than working very quickly and then having to stop and start again all the time.'

Michael says, 'I still think it's good to be quick. If the hare hadn't fallen asleep he would have won. We don't fall asleep in class do we?'

Sian responds to this. 'No, but we do other things – we stare out of the window, or talk to other people instead of getting on. That's being a hare.'

Jonathan says, 'Surely it's alright to talk to somebody else, and then make the time up afterwards?'

Michael says, 'I think so, too. We can't all plod steadily on all the time, never stopping, can we Miss?'

The teacher says, 'You are all correct, really. Notice that in the story the tortoise only just wins. That's important. It tells us that sprinting off and having a rest is OK, just so long as you know exactly what you are doing.

'Harold Hare made a mistake. Just a little quicker and it would have been a dead heat. And that might have been fair – there's more than one way of making progress in your work. Some people keep going steadily. Others go in little spurts. Either way is good if it gets the job done.

'The real difference between the hare and the tortoise is that while Timolena knew there was more than one way of winning, Harold was boastful and thought there was only his way. So he had to be taught a lesson.

'What Harold needed to realise was that the tortoise's slow and sure way of going about things was not something to laugh at. The

 ISBN 1 874050 55 4 pfp, 61 Gray's Inn Road, London WC1X 8TH

The Hare and the Tortoise

tortoise just had another way of doing things – and in the end it worked very well.

'Timolena Tortoise knew this. She knew that the hare was a fast runner. She also knew what she was good at. I'm not so sure about Harold. He knew what he was good at, but before the race he didn't really understand what Timolena was good at.

'It's important to learn two things, then. Firstly, to understand your own strengths and weaknesses. What are you good at? What are you not so good at? What could you do a little better?

'Second, you have to learn to recognise that if others do things differently, it may be because it's the best way for them, and it may be a better way than you think. If you watch and listen, you may learn something. Harold certainly learned something from his encounter with the tortoise. Never just assume that you are right and everyone else is wrong.'

A prayer

Lord, help us to accept the way that others do things, and not to believe that we are always right. Help us to be kind and supportive rather than boastful and selfish. Amen.

A thought

There's always more than one way of doing what has to be done.

Song suggestions

'Hands to Work and Feet to Run', *Someone's Singing Lord*, 21

'Same but Different', *Primary Assembly Song Book*, 52

Forgiveness

Assembly 1 of 4

This assembly considers a moral alternative to instant retaliation or the harbouring of grudges. In particular, it invites children to think about the motives and feelings of those who have offended.

You will need

- the OHT provided and a pen.

Taken by ....

Date ....

Given to ....

Comments

- ....
- ....
- ....

✦ Introduction

Who has a good friend? What do you like about your friend?

Put up OHT provided and write down the suggestions.

A friend is kind, thoughtful, funny, listens to you.

Take other suggestions and write them on the OHT provided.

When someone is like that, you feel very good about them. It makes you glad to see them. You see them coming in the distance and you wave and feel a bit better because they are there.

That's what it's like to have a good friend. Let's see if we can act out a meeting between friends.

Position two volunteers some distance apart.

Now walk slowly towards each other. There you go – walking along.

Then you see your friend in the distance. So you smile and wave. Then you shout, 'Hello!'

You run towards each other and stand telling each other all your news.

Just occasionally, though, something might go wrong. Let's act that out.

Position the two volunteers some distance apart again.

Now walk towards each other again – slowly like before. Now, let's change it this time.

Point at one volunteer.

One of you sees your friend in the distance. You smile and wave. But look!

Point at the other volunteer.

The other person, your friend, looks straight ahead and doesn't smile or wave. You walk straight past your friend, ignoring her completely.

How do you think you might feel if this happened to you? You would feel disappointed, let down and upset. Can you

 ISBN 1 874050 55 4

Forgiveness

think of any reason why your friend might have done this? Let's try to think of some reasons.

You might have upset your friend without knowing. Your friend might be upset about something else and be thinking so hard about it that she didn't see you.

Your friend might just not have seen you.

So what do you do about it?

You could get your own back of course. You could say, 'Next time I see my friend, I'm not going to speak. That will teach her!'

Would that be right? I don't think so.

You really want to put things right with your friend. Acting like that will just make things worse, not better. So what's the right thing to do?

First, you have to do something in your head. You have to put aside any angry feelings you have about your friend.

Then you have to find your friend and ask her why she did what she did. You listen to the explanation and you put things right with her so that you can return to being friends again. Your friend might say, 'Sorry.' If so, you should accept it and say, 'That's alright, I understand.'

Just suppose, though, that your friend really did intend to upset you.

Suppose it was like this. I'll tell you a little story to show what I mean.

Story

One day, Jane walked to school thinking about her friend Liz.

'I'm a bit fed up with Liz,' she thought. 'Sometimes she gets on my nerves with her giggling. I'll just ignore her today. That'll teach her not to get on my nerves.'

So when she saw Liz coming into the playground, she didn't run to meet her.

Instead, she pretended not to see her. She turned away and went to talk to someone else.

Afterwards, she thought that perhaps it was a silly thing to do. After all, Liz was a good friend.

'I wonder what Liz will do now,' she thought.

Pause.

Now let me stop there for a moment.

Let's think about what we said earlier. Suppose Liz had decided to get her own back.

Suppose Liz had said. 'Right! She ignored me, so I'm going to ignore her!'

That would have made things worse. Jane was already starting to wonder if she had done the right thing.

Luckily, Liz did not try to get her own back.

She went up to Jane at playtime and said, 'Why did you ignore me this morning? Didn't you see me?'

Of course, Jane could now do several things.

She could continue to ignore Liz and walk away. But she doesn't really want a big quarrel with Liz.

She could pretend that she didn't see Liz and say very casually, 'Sorry, Liz, I didn't see you.'

Would that be honest? No.

And it wouldn't be a wise thing to say, because Liz would probably know it was a lie. So there would still be a problem between Liz and Jane.

Good friends try to be truthful with each other. If friends feel that one is telling lies to the other, it spoils the friendship.

So this is what Jane did.

'Oh, Liz,' she said. 'I did a bad thing. I wanted to ignore you because I thought I was getting fed up with you. But once I had done it, I missed you and wanted to be friends again. Can you forgive me?'

Pause.

Think about that question – 'Can you forgive me?'

What does that mean?

To forgive someone is a generous act. It's a sort of giving, like giving a present.

Forgiving is not always easy.

It means that you know someone has done something wrong to you. Yet you say, 'That's alright. I won't carry the quarrel on. I will still be friends with you. I will try to understand what you did, and not let it affect my feelings.'

So Liz said, 'I forgive you, Jane. I want us to be friends still. Let's not say any more about it.'

Was that difficult for Liz? Perhaps. It depends on how angry she was. Or how badly she thought Jane had hurt her.

Forgiveness becomes really difficult when you have been badly and deliberately hurt by someone else.

Sometimes you hear people say, 'I'll never forgive him.'

And you can understand that, because some hurts are very bad and very difficult to forgive.

I'm not saying that you will always be able to forgive the hurts that are done to you. But we all have to try to look into ourselves to see whether we can forgive.

We have to stop and think.

Jane did something wrong. But she stopped before she went further. Liz thought about what to do and she stopped herself from making things worse.

Jane asked for forgiveness. And their friendship continued.

The incident gave them something to think about.

✦ Conclusion

Christians believe in trying to forgive. Jesus was quite clear. 'Forgive your enemies,' he said.

That's difficult. Jane and Liz were friends, not enemies. Forgiving an enemy is more difficult. I don't know how many people can do it.

But forgiveness is more likely to lead to peace and friendship than getting your own back is.

Forgiveness

A prayer

Dear God, we know you want us to forgive each other when we do wrong things to each other. You know we find that difficult.

Help us when we feel full of anger. Help us to stop, think and try to make good decisions that will bring us closer together rather than make thoughtless decisions that will drive us further apart.

Amen.

A thought

Forgive has the word 'give' in it. We all like to give presents and giving presents can make others happy too. We should try to 'give' forgiveness when things go wrong. Like giving presents, it can give us joy and bring friends closer to us.

Song suggestions

'Talking', *Tinderbox*, 52

'How we treat each other', *Primary Assembly Song Book*, 66

Optional follow up

Discuss similar situations the children have faced and how they dealt with them.

Choose words about friendship and display them. You could read *The Man* by Raymond Briggs (Red Fox 009910881X) for a range of emotions connected with friendship, including anger and jealousy.

A friend is

When I was a baby

Assembly 2 of 4

This assembly helps children to see how they have developed since they were born. In the story, a boy compares his abilities now with his abilities as a baby.

You will need

- some photographs of yourself, or someone else known to the pupils, as a baby.

Taken by ....

Date ....

Given to ....

Comments

- ....
- ....
- ....

✦ Introduction

Today we will be thinking about how we look back at things that once happened. How we can enjoy those memories and learn from them. We are also going to look the other way – we will see how we look forward to things that are still to come.

We're looking back to when *(I/name)* was a baby.

It was a long time ago.

Exaggerate here for a joke if you like.

Show the photographs.

We were all babies once. We had to be looked after then. There were things that we can do now that we couldn't do then. As time passes, we grow stronger and we can do more and more things.

Let's hear about growing up and learning more.

Story

One rainy day, Andrew was sitting with his grandad in the living room when Andrew's gran had gone out shopping.

They were wondering what to do for a change, when Andrew said, 'Let's look at some of the photographs.'

Andrew's gran was really good at looking after photographs. She took lots of them and when they came back from the chemist she would sort them out, put them in albums and then write something under every photograph.

'These are precious memories,' she would say. 'We need to know when and where the pictures were taken.'

As the years went by, she filled up her albums one by one. Gradually, the shelf behind the television was filled with a whole row of them.

Grandad said, 'Gran is really careful with her photo albums. She might tell us off if we have them out and start looking at them. She'll say we've got fingermarks on the pictures and got them out of order.'

'We'll wash our hands first,' said Andrew. 'Then we'll just get one album out and look at it.'

That is what they did. They washed their hands in the kitchen and dried them on a tea towel.

'Don't tell Gran!' whispered Grandad.

Then they went into the living room and Grandad chose a photo album from the shelf.

'This one!' he said. 'It has the pictures of you when you were a baby.'

Andrew settled down on the settee next to his grandad, who opened up the album across their laps.

'This is one of my favourites,' said Grandad, pointing to the picture on the first page. It was a picture of Andrew's gran, with a big smile on her face, holding a very tiny baby. In the background was a window ledge with a vase of flowers.

'That's in the hospital, the day you were born,' said Grandad.

'Is that me, then?' asked Andrew.

'That's you alright,' said Grandad. 'Less than a day old. Look how small you were. And look how big you are now!'

Andrew looked at the photograph for a few moments and then Grandad turned the page to a picture of Andrew on his own, still only a tiny baby, lying in a crib with his eyes closed.

'There you are again,' said Grandad. 'Still only a day old, in the hospital.'

Andrew looked again for a while. Then he said, 'I don't suppose I could do anything could I? I couldn't walk, or talk or anything?'

'Well I wouldn't say you couldn't do anything at all,' Grandad said. 'You cried quite a bit and waved your arms.'

'Why did I cry?' asked Andrew.

'Very small babies cry to let people know that they want food or that they are uncomfortable. It's the only way they can tell you these things.'

They continued to look through the album, turning the pages and enjoying the pictures. Many of them were of Andrew – sitting up in his pushchair, playing in the plastic paddling pool in Gran and Grandad's garden, toddling along pushing a toy dog on wheels.

Andrew looked at the pictures.

'First I could only cry. Then I could walk and talk,' he said.

His grandad nodded and said, 'Every day you made progress. First you could smile and recognise your mum. Then you could sit up. Soon you started reaching out for your favourite toys. Then you were crawling. You were into everything. You liked the pots and pans under the kitchen sink best. So your gran would let you get them out, then she would give you a wooden spoon to hit them with. You had a lovely time making a big noise!'

Andrew laughed. 'I still like making a noise!'

'But now,' said his grandad, 'you can make a lot of different noises. You can talk, shout, sing, play your recorder, clap your hands, bang up and down the stairs. And, of course, you can still laugh and cry.'

What else can I do now that I couldn't do then?' asked Andrew.

'Well think about it,' said Grandad. 'Look at this photograph of when you had just started

 ISBN 1 874050 55 4

to walk. You were thirteen months old. You could walk, but you could only just balance and sometimes you fell down on your bottom. You couldn't go up steps without someone helping you and you had to wave your arms around a lot to keep your balance.'

Andrew nodded and said, 'But now I can run up and down steps and I hardly ever fall over – just when I trip up over a ball.'

'You can get around in other ways too,' said Grandad. 'Can you think of anything?'

'I can ride my bike or go on my roller blades,' said Andrew. 'I couldn't do that when I was a baby could I?'

'No,' laughed Grandad. 'You had a little three wheeler, but you couldn't actually go anywhere on it. You just went round the garden a bit.'

'I've come on a lot!' said Andrew.

'That you have,' agreed Grandad. 'And you'll come on further still,' he added.

'How do you mean?' asked Andrew.

Grandad turned the pages of the photograph album until he came to empty ones near the end.

'Think what might be in here – you in your secondary school uniform. You playing guitar in a band. You with your friends at college. You getting married. Then you starting a photograph album of your own, with picture of your own little boy or girl in it.'

Andrew laughed. 'We'll look at it together, like we're looking at this one,' he said.

Grandad laughed too. 'I certainly hope so, Andrew. I really do.'

✦ Conclusion

All families watch their children grow and take delight in the progress that they make. They can also remember the earliest days.

Listen to what this middle-aged man wrote about his grown-up daughter.

'Today I went to the gym. I do that sometimes, just to keep my muscles and bones from seizing up. When I came out of the changing room, I looked at my watch. It was twelve o'clock.

'I realised that my daughter came to a class at the gym at 12.30. I thought it would be good just to say hello to her, so I got a cup of coffee from the bar and sat within sight of the door and read the paper for a while.

'Soon I was absorbed in a story in the paper. Then, suddenly, I heard a cheerful, 'Hello Dad!'

'I looked up and my daughter was coming through the door carrying her gym bag. She came across with a big smile on her face, glad to see me.

'I felt so proud of what she had become – a confident woman, living her own life, with a family of her own.

'But at the same time, for an instant, the years had rolled away.

'She was not thirty any more, but four years old, coming in from school with her Snoopy bag.

'It was a simple, everyday meeting and yet, for some reason, it seemed to be a special moment. I realised that my feelings for her were just the same now as they were then.

'Although she has made so much progress and is a mother herself now, she is still the little girl that I held in my arms all those years ago.'

A story about Jesus tells how his parents, Mary and Joseph were surprised at something he did as he grew.

The story says that as Jesus grew, he became very alert and wise. So much so, that on a visit to Jerusalem with his parents, he got lost for a while and they had to look for him.

They were really worried until they found him in the temple, talking and discussing with wise men.

They were worried, but they were also very proud that he was able to talk to the wise men in this way.

He had made great progress, but they still loved him because he was still the same child that they had watched over in that stable in Bethlehem.

None of you is very old really. All of you are still in single figures – less than ten years old. Yet look how far you have come in that time. Look at all the things you can do now that you couldn't do when you were a tiny baby.

A prayer

Dear God, we thank you for our growing strength in body and in mind. We thank you for all the care we have had from our families as we have grown. Help us as we continue to be stronger and wiser through the days and years to come. Amen.

A thought

By looking back at how we once were, we have an idea of how far we have come. By looking forward, we can see where we might be going.

Song suggestions

'I've got a memory of you', *Primary Assembly Song Book*, 47

'Jesus we are well and strong', *Someone's Singing Lord*, 40

Optional follow up

- Read the Bible story of Jesus in the temple in Luke, chapter 2, verses 40–52.
- Ask the children to bring in photographs of when they were babies and try to match the child and the baby photograph. You might include members of staff in this.

Voice of conscience

Assembly 3 of 4

This assembly is about the voice of conscience. A little girl wonders what it is and then experiences it in her own life.

You will need

- nothing at all.

Taken by ....

Date ....

Given to ....

Comments

- ....
- ....
- ....

✦ Introduction

This assembly is about listening to your own thoughts when they try to guide you and listening to the voices of friends and loved ones whose voices linger when they are no longer with us. We're looking back to when *(I/name)* was a baby.

Do you talk to yourself? Who does?

Well, I think everybody does. I certainly do. There are two ways of talking to yourself. One is to do it out loud. You might be trying to do a hard job and you say quietly to yourself, 'Come on, you can really do this if you try.'

Or you might talk to yourself without making a sound. You have the thoughts in your head, but the sounds don't come out.

So if you talk to yourself, can you listen to yourself? Of course you can. Thoughts come into your head – perhaps like voices – and you can listen to them. Have you ever heard a voice in your head say, 'Don't do it'? This story is about a girl who heard a voice putting her right about something she had done.

🕮 Story

Victoria asked her nan, 'How much room is there inside my head?'

Now Victoria's nan was used to difficult questions because Victoria wanted to know everything. Just over the last week Victoria had wanted to know where pepper comes from; the names of the Queen's corgis; why water only runs downhill; how many days there are in ten years; if there are English restaurants in China.

Her nan knew the answers to most of these – or at least she was able to find out because she was quite clever at finding things out.

This latest question, though, was something new. 'What was the question?' she said, looking puzzled.

'How much room is there inside my head?' asked Victoria again.

'Well, I don't think there's any room,' said Nan. 'Your head is full of your brain. There isn't any empty space in there as far as I know. Come here a minute.'

Voice of conscience

Victoria walked over to her nan.

Nan picked up the teaspoon from the saucer of her cup of tea and tapped Victoria lightly on the head with it.

'No,' she said. 'Sounds solid enough to me. No room for anything in there. No empty spaces. Why do you ask?'

Victoria replied, 'The curate came today, and he told us about doing wrong things and doing right things, and he said we had to listen to the voice of conscience. When Jo asked him where the voice was coming from, he said it was inside your head. So is there room for somebody with a voice inside your head?'

Victoria's nan laughed and answered, 'In fact, although your head is filled with brains, there's room for many voices in there. They don't take up any room, you see.'

'So what's the voice that the curate is on about then, Nan?' asked Victoria.

'Well, it's when you talk something over with somebody who's just in your mind. Or when you listen to somebody who is just in your mind,' replied Nan.

Victoria still looked puzzled, so Nan carried on.

'I live here on my own, don't I? Do you think I have nobody to talk to? In fact I have lots of people to talk to. I talk to your granddad, for one thing, even though he's not here any more. I asked him whether it would be right to move into an old people's bungalow, and I'm sure he told me that it was the right thing to do.'

'So the voice of conscience is granddad then?' asked Victoria.

Nan laughed again. 'Not really. Sometimes it's just a friend that you don't know, who keeps an eye on you.'

Victoria thought she knew what her nan meant, but she still wasn't sure.

The next day, when Victoria was walking to school, her mum asked, 'Victoria, you know those biscuits I got for Jimmy the other day?'

Victoria went red, because she knew what was coming next. Jimmy was a toddler that her mum looked after in the afternoons while his mum went to work. He loved biscuits. He would point to the biscuit tin and say, 'Biscuit!' – only not as clearly as that.

Victoria looked at her mum and grunted.

Her mum said, 'Well, when I came to give Jimmy a biscuit yesterday afternoon there weren't any left. I got the tin down and opened it without looking and held it down for him, and he put his little hand in and there weren't any in there. Can you imagine how he felt about that? He was quite upset really. Do you know anything about that?'

Victoria was quiet, but the voice inside her head wasn't quiet.

'Well, Victoria,' the voice seemed to say. 'I'm the friendly voice of conscience inside your head. Now it's time to listen to me.'

Victoria nodded, and her mum wondered why.

'Victoria,' said her friendly voice. 'You know what happened to those biscuits. The day before yesterday, when your mum was down the road taking Jimmy back to his mum, you opened the biscuit tin and finished them off. You thought your mum wouldn't notice. You thought that she'd think that she'd given them all to Jimmy. That's what you thought, wasn't it?'

Victoria nodded again. Her mum said, 'Why are you nodding, Victoria? Why don't you answer my question?'

Voice of conscience

Eventually, Victoria said, 'Well, I might have had a biscuit.'

Her mum nodded and the friend in Victoria's head said, 'Well done so far, now keep going.'

She carried on, 'I might have eaten all the biscuits. Really, I did eat all the biscuits. I had one, and then I kept having another. Sorry, Mum.'

Her mum stopped and turned to Victoria.

'So Jimmy had no biscuits,' she said. 'I'm sorry too. But I'm glad you told me what happened. So it's no biscuits for you until the weekend. You've had your share. OK?'

The voice of the imaginary friend inside her head said, 'Yes. I think you did the right thing there, Victoria.' Victoria nodded in agreement.

✦ Conclusion

Was there a real person inside Victoria's head? I don't think so. So who could she hear? Well, I think it was her own thoughts. It was nothing magic and nothing to worry about. You see, the voice didn't tell Victoria anything she didn't already know, so it was her own thoughts that she was listening to. She was thinking out what she had done, and she decided to do the right thing. She listened to her thoughts and made a good decision.

A prayer

Dear God, we thank you for our ability to think things through and decide on what is right and wrong. Help us to listen to the voice of conscience and to put things right when we have made a wrong choice. Amen.

A thought

The voice of conscience is really our own thoughts, but we still need to listen. Too often we don't take notice of our own thoughts.

Song suggestions

'My little island', *Primary Assembly Song Book*, 88

'Think on these things', *Someone's Singing Lord*, 38

Optional follow up

Encourage the children to think about their own times of listening to their deeper thoughts, building on the examples in the assembly. Discuss them and then allow time for writing them down.

Who am I?

Assembly 4 of 4

Becoming a spiritual person implies learning who you are. Here a young child looks at her favourite things in her room and thinks of what they mean to her. She also looks in a mirror and thinks about who she is and how other people may see her.

You will need

- a mirror
- some favourite things of your own that you can talk very briefly about.

Taken by ....

Date ....

Given to ....

Comments

- ....
- ....
- ....

✦ Introduction

In this assembly we will think about who we are and what we are like. You may think you know that already – you know who you are, don't you? Of course you do. But sometimes we spend so much time looking at others and talking to them that we don't get time to think about what we are like ourselves. This assembly will help us to do that.

Look in the mirror.

Who's that staring back at me? Why, it's me of course! It's a very familiar face. I see it every morning, and I see it at other times in the day. Sometimes I see it in a photograph, or even on a video.

So I know who it is in the mirror, don't I? That face belongs to me. There are other things that are mine, too, that I can't see in the mirror. There are my thoughts and my feelings. They belong to me, and they're different from yours.

Sometimes you can understand your own feelings and thoughts a bit better if you have something to remind you of them.

Look at these things of mine.

Say a word or two about them and what they mean to you. For example, a photograph of your children might remind you that as well as being a teacher or a head, you are a father or mother, with all the feelings and responsibilities that go with those things.

So you know who you are? Of course you do. You are somebody's son or daughter, and you are a pupil at this school. You have a face that's different from everyone else's and you have thoughts and feelings that are different from everyone else's.

You have to learn that, though. You have to learn to know yourself, and it's not as easy as it seems.

Think about a baby, for example. Most of you have seen a baby, at home or in someone else's house.

Who am I?

Have you noticed that when a baby starts to talk, he doesn't start by saying his own name. He says a much more important word. What does he usually say first? That's right, he says 'Mummy'.

Mummy is very real you see – an important person who gives love and care. The baby can reach out and touch Mummy's face, and smile at her.

Then, after a while, the baby will say another person's name – 'Daddy' perhaps, or 'Granny'. And he might have a go at his brother or sister's name if it's not too hard.

But have you noticed that it's a long time before he says his own name. It's some time before he knows that the person in the mirror is himself.

We've all been babies, of course. And so we all learned about other people before we learned about ourselves. We knew that our mums were kind to us long before we knew whether we were kind people or not. We understood lots of things about other people before we understood them about ourselves.

Now let's meet Rachel, who's in her room thinking about herself and who she is.

Story

Rachel's room is a small room, with a small bed, a small chair, and a small dressing table. Although it's small, it's filled with lots of things. And because it's Rachel's room, the things in it are Rachel's.

When we meet Rachel, she's just being in her room, sitting on her bed, looking around at her things.

What she likes about her things is that each one of them tells a story. What does that mean? Well, it doesn't mean that it stands up on little legs and starts talking to her. It means that each of her things reminds her of times and places and people.

The first thing that Rachel looked at that Saturday morning was her shelf with her videos on it. Rachel likes her videos. She can't watch them in her room. She has to wait until her mum will put them on for her downstairs. But she likes to have them in her room because – well, because they're her very own, and because they look colourful all in a row on the shelf. She also likes to have them there because she can take them down and look at the pictures on the boxes, and read the words. Some of them are nearly as good as a picture book.

Now, let's see Rachel as she gets up and walks across to her videos. She picks up *Fun Song Factory* and sits down on the bed again to look at it.

She's had *Fun Song Factory* for a long time. Her mum says Rachel used to watch it with her brother before she could walk or talk. Sometimes her mum is surprised that she still likes it, but she really does. She likes all of the songs – 'I Went to Visit a Farm', 'Incy Wincy Spider', 'The Wheels on the Bus' and all the others, and she still does the actions to herself when she watches it.

Rachel sits looking at her video for a while. She thinks how much she likes the songs on it, and for a while she sings some of them silently in her head. 'I like singing, and I like songs,' she says to herself.

And as she looks at the video, some memories come into her mind of the times that she has watched it with other people. She remembers sitting with her grandad watching the video and singing the songs with him. That's one good memory, and it reminds her that she is her grandad's granddaughter.

Then she remembers standing in the living room watching the video and doing the actions with her cousin Tom. That's another good memory and it reminds her that she is part of a big family with lots of cousins.

Most of all she remembers going to the theatre when the *Fun Song Factory* came there, with real people on the stage, and she sat all the way through just amazed by it.

That's a very good memory that comes into her mind as she sits looking at the video in her hands. It reminds her how she started to think, 'I'm going to be on the stage one day.'

Soon after she saw the show, she started to have dancing lessons. 'I'm a person who goes to dancing lessons,' she thought to herself, 'because I want to be a dancer on the stage one day.'

Rachel puts down her *Fun Song Factory* video and looks around. Then she spots Eric, her panda. Eric is a soft toy, with a knitted body. Every night he sleeps in her bed, and every night she cuddles up with him. Eric has been with her as long as she can remember. Mum said that her Aunt Joan bought it for her when she was first born. He's a battered panda now. One ear's nearly chewed off and he's grey where he's supposed to be white. But he's still old Eric.

Rachel picks Eric up and sits looking at him for a while, and lots of memories come into her mind.

She remembers how she left Eric behind once, when they went on holiday, and her dad had to come all the way back from the seaside for him because she missed him so much. That was a good memory. It made her think how much her dad loves her. She thinks of how her big brother likes to have a secret cuddle with Eric when he thinks nobody is looking.

As she sits on the bed, Rachel notices herself in the mirror. She stares at herself for a while, turning her head from side to side and trying to look at herself sideways out of the corner of her eye. People say she looks like her dad. Others say she looks like her mum. She doesn't know really. But she does know that she's someone who likes to sing songs and have dancing lessons and wants to go on the stage. She knows she's part of a big family, with lots of cousins and a grandad. And she knows that her dad and all her family love her.

She keeps on looking at herself and tries to imagine what she might be like when she is as old as her mum. Sometimes her mum lets her try on a bit of lipstick. When she does that, Rachel and her mum look in the mirror together.

Her mum might say, 'I used to look like that once, trying on some of my mum's lipstick. You're just like I used to be.'

Rachel thinks about that, and she holds on to Eric, and walks over to the mirror. She looks into it for a long time. Then she speaks.

'Hi,' she says quietly. 'I'm Rachel.'

Rachel is learning a lot about herself. She knows that she likes singing and dancing and is starting to think that she might like to do more of it when she grows up. She knows that she likes her cuddly toy, partly because it reminds her of holidays, and her mum and

Who am I?

dad, and her brother. She knows that the people in her family love her. She has a good idea of what she looks like because she is looking in a mirror, but she knows that the mirror doesn't really tell her what other people see. She learns these things almost without knowing it from the people around her, and she thinks about them when she is on her own.

✦ Conclusion

Do you have favourite things that remind you of other people and other times?

What do you know about yourself? I guess you know the things that you like best and who your friends are. I wonder, though, whether you know what other people think of you? Do they think you are funny? Do they think you are kind? How do you know what they think of you?

People of all religions believe that self knowledge is important. Religious leaders tell us to think how we would like to be treated, and then treat other people like that.

If you understand your own feelings, and if you can look in the mirror and see the person behind the face, then you will be better at getting on with other people. Other people know you very well. What kind of person is it that they know? Have you thought about that?

A prayer

Lord, help me to think about the kind of person I am. Help me to know my likes and dislikes, and to know the good things about myself and the not-so-good – because then you can help me to put the not-so-good things right. Amen.

A thought

Other people seem very real to you – a kind person, a funny person, someone you love, someone you hardly know. Now, as you grow, you are learning about yourself, still a stranger in some ways. Try always to be a person that you like.

Song suggestions

'He gave me eyes so I could see,' *Tinderbox* 19

'My little island,' *Primary Assembly Song Book* 88

Optional follow up

Write the words 'I am a person who likes…' and then make a list of all the things you like, and the things you like to do. Then write 'I am a person who does not like…' and make a list of all the things you don't like and the things you don't like to do.

Stick your lists together, and put a photograph of yourself with them.

Seeing is believing

Assembly 1 of 4

This assembly deals with the doubts of the disciple Thomas, who would not believe in the resurrection until he had seen Jesus for himself. It tries to present young children with the idea that belief and trust are important.

You will need

- a blank OHT and a pen.

Taken by ....

Date ....

Given to ....

Comments

- ....
- ....
- ....

✦ Introduction

Call a volunteer out to the front. (Choose someone who is fairly confident under gentle pressure.)

Hello, who are you?

When he or she replies, ask, 'How do I know?'

Deal with whatever answer the child comes up with. Then ask the whole group, 'How do I know this is *(name)*?'

Who can tell me how we know this is her? Can we write some reasons up on the OHT?

Suggestions may include 'it looks like her', 'we remember what she looks like, 'she says it's her.

Does anyone know people in school who look like each other?

Children will usually come up with answers. They often all agree on which of their friends look like each other. They may, of course, choose a pair of twins.

Can we have those two up to the front? Now. Can you tell me who is who? This is...? And this is...? How do we know?

Discuss how we can tell the difference between them. If appropriate, write some characteristics on the OHT.

Now who'll go out of the room and pretend to have been away for a long time?

Choose a volunteer and send them out.

Now, we're going to count ten years. Here goes – count with me, one, two, three...

Right, ask *(name)* to come back in.

Pretend not to recognise her.

Hello, who are you? Are you a new pupil? Who did you say you were? How do I know? She went away a long time ago. I don't think you are her at all.

I won't believe it's *(name)* until somebody proves it to me. Tell you what. The *(name)* that I used to know was very good at *(choose something that the child really is good at – reading, jumping, whatever)*.

Right, let's see if you can do it?

Carry out the test.

Very well, I believe it's you now!

Seeing is believing

What happened then? I gave *(name)* a test to see if it really was her. But it would have been better if I had trusted her, wouldn't it? If she said she was *(name)* then I ought to have trusted her and not made her do a test.

The New Testament tells us about somebody who couldn't believe that somebody was who he said he was.

Story 1

After Jesus rose from the tomb in the garden on the first Easter Day, he came to see his followers one day. They were having a meeting. They had the door locked because they were afraid of being captured like Jesus had been. Jesus came and stood among them and said, 'Peace be with you!'

The disciples believed it really was Jesus, even though they had seen him crucified and they were really excited. Thomas, one of Jesus's followers, wasn't there, and when they saw him they said. 'Thomas! We have seen the Lord!'

'I don't believe you!' said Thomas. 'He was crucified. You can't have seen him!'

The other friends of Jesus tried to persuade Thomas, but he wouldn't believe them. 'Sorry. I'll have to see him myself. It's no good you just telling me.'

Thomas was really shocked when Jesus was captured and crucified. He thought all Jesus's good work was finished. He was very upset and feeling very low. So he really didn't believe what the others told him. He thought it must have been some sort of vision, or that they were so upset they would believe anything.

A week later, the followers were having another meeting and again the doors were locked because they were afraid of being arrested.

Then Jesus appeared again among them. This time Thomas was there, and saw him.

Jesus said, 'Peace be with you!'

Jesus asked Thomas to come closer and see how his hands had been hurt when he was crucified. 'Now do you believe it's me, Thomas?' he asked.

Thomas said, 'My Lord and my God!'

Jesus told Thomas that it was all very well to see and believe but it was much better to believe without seeing.

This is an important Christian message. We cannot see God. We can no longer see Jesus. We cannot do what Thomas did and ask to see him before we believe. Christians are asked to believe in God and in the love of Jesus without seeing him. That's not easy.

But there are things that we can see. We can see the beauty of the world. We can hear the beauty of our friends' voices and the sound of music. We can feel the love of our friends and families. All of this love comes from God. We believe in it. It is very real to us, and very important. Thomas didn't just see Jesus. He felt the love of Jesus that he had known for so long.

People who have a deep religious belief – whether they are Christians, Muslims, Sikhs, Hindus or Buddhists – all believe things they cannot see. But the feelings inside them are very real. They understand the words of Jesus, who said that it is important to believe without seeing. Here's another story.

Story 2

When Kirsty's grandad died, she was very upset. She missed him very much because he used to play with her a lot and take her for walks. Ever since she could remember, Kirsty's grandad had always been there. Now he suddenly wasn't there any more.

Kirsty was very quiet after her grandad's funeral. Her mum knew that she was upset but Kirsty wasn't talking much and her mum was upset herself so she didn't say much to Kirsty.

Then it was the Easter holidays and Kirsty didn't have to go to school for a bit. On the first day of the holiday, she said to her mum, 'Is it Good Friday tomorrow?'

'Yes, Kirsty, it is.'

'And will it be Easter Day on Sunday?'

'Yes, Kirsty, it will be.'

'And was Jesus crucified on Good Friday, and then came alive again on Easter Day?'

'That's what Christians believe, Kirsty.'

'Well, Mum, if Jesus came alive again, why can't Grandad come alive again?'

Kirsty's mum thought about this for a bit. It was a hard question.

'Jesus was sent by God to do a special job. He died for all of us and then he came from the tomb to show that death hadn't won.'

'But Grandad was special too. Can't God bring him back?'

'Perhaps Grandad is with God. I really don't know. I do know that we won't see him again here with us. But that doesn't mean that he's completely gone.'

'What do you mean?' asked Kirsty.

'Your grandad loved us very much. He loved you specially, because you were his only granddaughter. All of that love can't just disappear. You can think about your grandad and feel the love he had for you, can't you? And you can talk about him to me, and we can remember him. He won't come back to us so that we can see him. But he hasn't just left an empty space behind, has he?'

Kirsty still wasn't sure.

'Well, we didn't go to see him every day, did we? On the days when we didn't go, we didn't stop thinking about him, did we? We didn't stop loving him on those days. And he didn't stop loving us. Just think of it like that. Just think that he's there really but we're not going to see him today. Every day will be like that. But we will think of him and be grateful to God that he spent so much time with us.'

Kirsty felt a bit better after that. She was still sad but she was also glad that she could think about her grandad without being quite so upset.

A prayer

Dear God, the message of Easter isn't always easy to understand. We just have to accept it. We know that you love us, and we know that the love we have for each other is part of your love for us. Help us to believe even though we cannot see and even though we cannot completely understand. Amen.

A thought

When someone goes out of the room, we don't forget them straightaway. They are there in our minds. We can see them. We can pretend to talk to them and we know what they would say to us. If we reach out we might almost touch them.

Song suggestions

'Put your hand', *Alleluya*, 40
'A man for all the people', *Come and Praise*, 27
'We have a King', *Someone's Singing Lord*, 51

Pandora's box

Assembly 2 of 4

This is an assembly for infants based on the legend of Pandora's box. It explores the idea of bad and good feelings and how we can try to control the quality of the feelings inside us.

You will need

- a cardboard box – big enough to look interesting
- some sticky tape and string to seal the box up with later
- big sheets of paper (or an OHT) with a drawing of a box, with room for writing inside
- an OHP and pens
- a chair.

Taken by ....

Date ....

Given to ....

Comments

- ....
- ....
- ....

✦ Introduction

Have you seen my lovely box? I wonder what's inside it? You can get all sorts of things into a box. At Christmas or for your birthday, you sometimes get good things in boxes.

The thing about a box, though, is that when someone gives you one, you really want to open it. Just suppose I gave one of you this box and asked you to look after it for a few days. You'd be dying to know what was in it, wouldn't you? You might even try to peep inside or open it. You might work out whether you could open it and then seal it up again without me knowing.

Now I'm going to tell you a very old story about a mysterious box, and about Pandora who had to look after it but wasn't allowed to look inside.

Story

Once, there was a beautiful person called Pandora. Every day she went for a walk in the woods near her home. Everything was beautiful around her as she walked – the trees were green; the flowers were sweet smelling and colourful. Rabbits and squirrels played around her as she walked. The world was beautiful then, with nothing at all to spoil it. And as Pandora walked, she would often talk to herself and sing.

One day, as she was walking and singing, she heard a voice calling in the distance. 'Pandora! Pandora! Can I trust you?' it called.

She stopped and looked around, but there was nothing, only the breeze in the trees and the singing of the birds and the rustling of rabbits in the undergrowth. So she walked on, still singing and talking to herself. Then she heard it again. 'Pandora! Pandora! Can I trust you?' it called again.

This time she stopped and answered, calling out, 'Who is that? Who knows my name? Who is calling me?'

She listened for an answer but once again there was nothing, only the breeze in the trees and the singing of the birds and the rustling of rabbits in the undergrowth. So she walked on, still singing and talking to herself.

Then, for a third time, she heard the voice again. 'Pandora! Pandora! Can I trust you?' it said.

Once again, Pandora stopped and asked, 'Who is that? Who knows my name? Who is calling me?'

For a moment, the woods were still quiet, except for the breeze in the trees and the singing of the birds and the rustling of rabbits in the undergrowth.

Then, walking towards her, she saw a man dressed in a long white robe. Behind him walked two other men. On their shoulders they carried a long pole. Hanging from the pole was a great wooden box. 'Pandora! Pandora!' called the man. 'Here I am,' replied Pandora.

The little procession – the man in white and the men carrying the box – made their way through the woods until they stood before Pandora. The man in white spoke again.

'Pandora, I have chosen you to look after this precious and very special box. It is to stay in your house for ever. You must look after it very carefully, but you are never, never to open it,' he said. 'But why have you chosen me?' asked Pandora.

'Because you live alone and you are a good person. I think we can trust you with our precious box,' replied the man.

'But what is in the box that is so special and precious?' asked Pandora.

'That I cannot tell you. It is a secret for ever. But you must never ever look inside. If you look inside you will spoil everything for everybody in the whole world,' he replied. 'Very well then,' said Pandora. 'Bring the box to my house.'

Pandora turned and the procession walked through the woods to her house. Pandora led the way, the man in white came next and the two men carrying the box followed on behind. As they walked, the breeze moved the trees, the birds sang and the rabbits rustled in the undergrowth.

Soon they came to Pandora's little cottage in the woods. They went inside, and Pandora pointed to a corner by the hearth. 'The box can go here,' she said.

The two men put the box down and unfastened the ropes that were carrying it. Then they stepped back.

The man in white stood by the box and spoke to Pandora.

'Now remember, Pandora, that you must take care of the box. You must not open it, ever. You must not even peep inside. If you look you will see that it has a handle on the front. There is no lock. If you were to turn the handle, you could easily lift the lid and look inside. But you are not to do it. We have chosen you because we trust you.'

Pandora's box

Pandora was very puzzled but she agreed, and the party of men left and walked off into the woods.

Pandora waved to the men from the door, then she went back inside. She stood and looked at the box. 'I wonder what's inside it?' she thought. 'What can be so important? Why can't I have a look?' Then she shrugged her shoulders. She decided to forget about the box and get on with things.

But every day, her curiosity grew. She would go up to the box and put her hand on the lid. Once, she bent down and put her ear to the box and listened carefully. Perhaps she could just hear a very faint murmuring – a sort of very quiet buzzing noise, as if there were bees or birds in the far distance. But then she thought that she was imagining it, or perhaps it was just the noises that you hear if you put a cup or a seashell to your ear.

Every day, Pandora went to the box. What could be inside? Sometimes she sat on the lid and just thought about it. Sometimes she walked up and down in front of it. Sometimes she just put her hands on it and tried to feel what was inside. But that was no good of course, because you really can't feel through a wooden box.

Then, one morning, she said to herself. 'Perhaps if I just turn the handle, that would not do any harm, would it?'

She sat for a while in a chair, looking at the box. Then, quite suddenly, she stood up and walked across the room to the box and, without hesitating, she turned the handle. It was a lovely brass handle in the shape of a dragon.

It turned very easily, just as if it had been oiled. She heard the catch slide back inside the lid. And just for a moment, she thought she heard the murmuring inside grow louder. It was only for a second and then it went away again.

After she had turned the handle, she did not open the box. She went and sat down again and stared at the box across the room.

The man in white had said that it would spoil everything if she opened the box. But how could it? How could just looking inside do any harm. She wouldn't even get anything out. She wouldn't even put her hands in or move anything. She wouldn't even open the lid completely, she would just open it a bit and then she would bend down and peep. How could that do any harm?

Pandora had made up her mind. She stood up, walked across to the box again, kneeled down beside it, put her two hands on the edge of the lid and gently lifted it. It moved very easily, just as the handle had done. Slowly the lid came up, and Pandora put her head forward to look inside. All was darkness in the little crack that she had opened. She bent further, and leaned forward to peep inside.

Suddenly, there was a bang and a terrible noise and Pandora fell backwards. The lid of the box had been snatched from her hands and had been flung right back, completely open. There was a great rushing sound and a big and terrible darkness, like the thickest smoke you could imagine came rushing from the box. It roared out, a great thick stream, across the room and out of the door of Pandora's house. For several minutes it roared on, thick darkness flowing through Pandora's house and out into the woods. Then, gradually, it became thinner, and slower and quieter, bit by bit until finally it stopped and all was quiet again.

Pandora sat quite still. She was very frightened. What had she done? What had happened? Fearfully, she got to her feet and went across to the box. She looked inside. It was completely empty – bare as bare could be, neat and clean inside as the day that it was made. What had been inside it? What was so important?

As she looked, a shadow fell across her, and she turned. Standing in the doorway was the man in white who had left the box with her. He was shaking his head.

'Oh, Pandora, Pandora, what have you done? I trusted you not to open the box,' he said.

'But I only wanted a little look! I didn't know what would happen,' Pandora replied.

'I chose you because I trusted you,' said the man.

Pandora hung her head in shame. 'What was in the box?' she asked.

'We have a lovely world. All is goodness and beauty. That was because all the bad things were in the box – all the bad feelings, all the bad things that people do. All were in the box. Now you have let them out, and the world will never be the same again,' he replied sadly.

Pandora went slowly to the door and looked out. The woods looked much the same, but the birds were not singing so loudly and the rabbits seemed to have gone back to their burrows. Pandora knew that things would not be the same again.

The man in white spoke. 'Look again in the box, Pandora, and perhaps things are not quite so bad as we think.'

'But the box is empty now,' said Pandora.

But she went to look all the same and sure enough, in a corner of the box, there was a small glowing jewel. She was sure it had not been there before. How could she have missed it?

'What is it?' she asked.

'It is the hope of the world. The most precious thing we have is hope – that bad things can be defeated and that good can win over evil. Now we must release hope from the box too,' the man in white replied.

Pandora reached into the box and picked up the jewel. She held it in her two hands, and it glowed through her fingers and lit up her face.

She carried it to the door, looked at it for a moment, and then drew back her arms and threw it with all her strength towards the woods. It shone and sparkled in the air, rising first, and then falling towards the trees. Then, just as it was going to fall into the woods, it vanished suddenly. In its place there was a white dove. The beautiful bird flapped its wings, climbed away from the woods, circled for a moment and then flew off towards the distant horizon.

The man in white put his hand on Pandora's shoulder and together they watched it until it was no more to be seen.

Pandora's box

✦ Conclusion

That is the ancient story of Pandora's box. Long ago, people told the story to explain how bad things and bad feelings came into the world.

Show cardboard box. Now let's look at our box. Just suppose we had the chance to collect up all sorts of bad things and put them in the box – bad feelings and thoughts. What could we put in?

Take suggestions and write them on the box. These might include jealousy, bullying, name-calling. Take as many as seem appropriate. Then pick up the cardboard box.

This box has all the bad things that you told me. Shall we seal it up now?

Make a big show of sealing up the box with sellotape (and string if you have some).

Now, we've sealed up nasty things in this box. Let's see if we can leave them there.

Optional

Later, the box could be appropriately labelled and put on display. It could be referred to or used as a focus for discussion when incidents occurred in school.

Now let's look at the box on the *(OHT/paper)*. Let's think of as many good things as we can to put in this box.

Take suggestions and write them on the OHT/paper.

A prayer

Dear God, we thank you for all the good things in our lives.

Invite the children to say with you the good things that are listed on the box on the OHT/paper.

We thank you for... We thank you for... We ask for you help when we meet things that are not so good – unkindness, unhappiness. Keep us safe today; keep all the good things that we have breathed in working well inside us. Amen.

A thought

Let's say together the good things that we have written on the OHT. We'll say them slowly, and have a little think after each of them. Think how each of them works in your own life. Who is kind to you? How can you be kind to others? Think of each one like that. Now let's say them.

Song suggestions

'Talking', *Tinder Box*, 52

'Look out for loneliness', *Someone's Singing Lord,* 36

It makes me angry

Assembly 3 of 4

This assembly is about three children from the same family, making a fresh start at new schools. It shows that it's quite normal to be worried about big changes in life. It offers reassurance that when changes come along, there are people ready to help.

You will need

- nothing at all.

Taken by ....

Date ....

Given to ....

Comments

- ....
- ....
- ....

✦ Introduction

In this assembly we're going to think about what makes us angry and how anger affects us. We will think about how we can deal with these feelings so that they do not make us or other people unhappy.

Have you ever wanted to do something really badly, and your parents wouldn't let you do it?

I know I have. *Provide an example from your own childhood.*

How do you feel when that happens? Frustrated? Angry?

What's the usual thing that you want to say when that happens? That's right. You want to say, 'It's not fair!'

Sometimes, though, it's you that's not being fair. You haven't thought about why you're not being allowed to do what you want to do. There might be good reasons. Your parents might not be able to afford it for one thing. If they can't afford it, it's you that's not being fair if you keep asking. Or they might think that what you want to do is not safe. If they think that, then it's not fair of you to keep wanting to do something dangerous.

Usually, after being disappointed for a while, you think about things and then you realise that you shouldn't have been so angry. That's what happened to Rhian in this story.

🕮 Story

Dad had made up his mind. 'For the last time, Rhian,' he said, 'you cannot go up to the shop on your own with Simone, and that's final. Don't ask again.'

Rhian had been on about it all morning. Simone was a bit older than her, and her mum let her go up to the corner shop on her own, even though it meant crossing the main road at the traffic lights. Dad thought that Rhian was too young to do it, even with Simone, and so he just said no.

Rhian thought this was very unfair. Simone was only just a bit older then her, and in any case, she thought, Simone would be able to look after her.

It makes me angry

Dad thought differently. What Simone's mum let Simone do was up to Simone's mum, but he didn't really think that Simone would be able to look after Rhian. No, he wasn't going to allow it to happen. So that was that. End of story.

Rhian didn't see it like that though.

'Dad...' she said. But she didn't get any further.

'RHIAN!' he said in a very loud voice. 'THAT... IS... ENOUGH.'

At that, Rhian really went mad. She cried, she screamed, she flopped in the chair with her head in her hands. She said it wasn't fair. She wanted to know why other people could do things and she couldn't.

Her dad just walked out of the room and slammed the door. 'I'll talk to you when you are ready to talk properly,' he said, and he went into the kitchen and did a lot of banging about with the pots and pans.

Rhian sobbed to herself. Life was so unfair, she thought. All she wanted was to go down to the shop with her friend. Why was that so terrible? Simone could go. Why couldn't she go?

'It's just not fair,' she said aloud – but not so loud that her dad could hear. She didn't want to set him off again.

In the end she went up to her room and flopped on her bed and started to read a book.

After half an hour there was a little knock on the door, and her dad put his head round and looked at her.

'Calmed down yet?' he asked.

Rhian stuck her bottom lip out and just looked at him.

He came and sat beside her on the bed.

'Now you've quietened down a bit,' he said, 'let's have a talk and see why you got so angry. And why I got angry too, because we both did. Now, tell me why you got angry.'

Rhian sat quietly for a while. Then she said, 'Because you wouldn't let me go to the shop with Simone.'

'That's right,' said Dad. 'Now tell me why I wouldn't let you go.'

That was more difficult, but she remembered in the end.

'Because you thought Simone might not look after me properly, and I'm younger than her.'

'Right,' said Dad. 'So for me it was like letting you go on your own. It wouldn't have been fair to expect Simone to look after you. Now think. Have you ever been down to the shops on your own? I'm not even sure you'd be happy going down there on your own. Would you?'

Rhian thought for a bit, then she shook her head. Her dad was right. She probably wouldn't want to go down to the shops on her own. So that meant she probably shouldn't go down with Simone, because Simone was not really old enough to look after her if anything went wrong.

Rhian's dad sat on the bed with her and put his arm round her. 'I got mad as well, Rhian. Sometimes you wind me up when you get in a tantrum like that.'

'But we're still friends,' said Rhian.

'Oh yes,' said Dad. 'Always friends. No matter what.'

It makes me angry

'Dad,' said Rhian, 'what do we get angry for? Why do we have a thing called being angry?'

Her dad laughed, and then thought for a moment. 'That's a good question. There are times when it can be useful of course. If someone is doing the wrong thing and treating you very badly, then you may well feel very angry. And that can give you the courage to do something about it – to speak up or to tell someone. But feeling angry isn't the same as having a tantrum and shouting and screaming. What happens is you feel angry, and then you decide to control it and not let it control you. If you have a screaming tantrum then the anger is controlling you. It's a bit like a wild animal inside that's taken over. What you have to do is keep it tame and under control.'

'I think Mum does that,' said Rhian.

Dad laughed again. 'She certainly keeps very calm when she's annoyed,' he said.

Rhian nodded. 'She gets quieter instead of louder, and her eyes go narrow. But she doesn't shout. She just talks very quietly. She did it to that man in the electrical shop the other day.'

'Oh yes,' said Dad. 'We can learn a lot about controlled anger from your mum.'

✦ Conclusion

It's not wrong to be angry. All religious leaders have been angry whenever they have come up against something they believed to be wrong. When Jesus found people buying and selling and lending money in the temple in Jerusalem, he was very angry indeed.

'You have made God's house into a den of thieves,' he said.

No, when it's wrong is when you lose control of yourself and start shouting and having a tantrum. Losing control of your own feelings is never a good thing to do, and it doesn't achieve what you want either.

A prayer

Lord, help us to understand when life goes against us. And if we feel angry, help us to keep control and to channel our feelings so that they work for us and not against us. Amen.

A thought

A storm blowing inside, but calm on the outside – that's what we should aim at.

Song suggestions

'How we treat each other', *Primary Assembly Song Book* 6

'When a knight won his spurs', *Someone's Singing Lord,* 34

Optional follow up

Make a list of the times you've been stopped from doing something you wanted to do. Then think about each one. Was it right that you were stopped? If so, put a tick beside it.

I love my new brother, but…

'We're bound to spend a lot of time with baby Jack, Rosie. But we want you to remember that you are very special to us. We'll always love you very much.'

I love my new brother, but…

Assembly 4 of 4

In this assembly a girl tries to sort out her feelings towards her newborn brother. She loves him, but she has to come to terms with the demands that he will make upon her parents' time.

Caution – take care if there is a child in your school whose sibling has not been born healthy.

You will need

- the OHT provided.

Taken by ....

Date ....

Given to ....

Comments

- ....
- ....
- ....

✦ Introduction

In our assembly we are going to talk about loving each other. It's a complicated feeling sometimes, as Rosie discovers in today's story.

Who's had a new baby in their house? Can you remember how you felt? Perhaps you felt a mixture of things – love and excitement. And perhaps you felt just a bit put out by all the attention the baby was getting – people making a fuss of the baby and not you.

Now that's why love can be a complicated business. It would be much easier to love the new baby, or anyone at all, if they didn't cause you any hard work or trouble. But the whole point of loving someone is that your love is stronger than any problems that the loved one might cause. It's not put off when things go wrong.

Love is something that you give without asking anything in return. It's a gift, like a birthday present, but it comes from you all the time, and not just on special occasions.

In this story, Rosie comes to find those things out when she thinks about loving her new baby brother.

🕮 Story

Rosie lay awake in her little bed in her room at the back of the house. It had been a big and important week. One week ago, there had been only three people in the house, Rosie and her mum and dad. Tonight there were four, Rosie and her mum and dad and a baby called Jack.

When her mum had told her, quite a long time ago, that she was going to have a baby and that Rosie was going to have a brother or sister, she hadn't really known what to think. One thing she certainly did think, though, and that was that her mum would be going to hospital to have the baby. Everyone went to hospital to have babies, didn't they? It definitely happened like that on television. The woman having the baby would have a pain, and then she'd have to be taken off to hospital in a rush, and there'd be a lot of fuss and groaning, and nurses and doctors and dad

 ISBN 1 874050 55 4 pfp, 61 Gray's Inn Road, London WC1X 8TH

I love my new brother, but...

getting in a state, and then there'd be a little baby, all wrinkled and new looking and everyone would smile and say 'ah'.

Her mum, though, had wanted something different. It was just like her, Rosie thought. She always wanted to do things her way. That's why they went to little cottages in the countryside for their holidays instead of to hot beaches in Spain like normal people. Rosie smiled when she thought of some of those rainy holidays. And if the truth were known, the reason she smiled was because she enjoyed those holidays, just with her mum and dad, playing games, having fun, trying to cook, exploring woods and playing at outlaws and aliens and things and laughing all the time.

So, her mum, who always wanted to do something different, was going to have her baby at home.

'Everybody had their baby at home once upon a time,' said Mum, when Dad protested. 'It's a normal thing to have a baby. It's not an illness, and I'm not going to hospital. I'll have my baby here with the midwife and you helping me. Everything will be alright.'

And so it was. A week ago, Rosie had been woken in the night by voices and bumping and banging. Then her dad had popped his head round the door. 'Are you awake, Rosie?' her dad had said. 'It's OK, the midwife's coming. I think there's going to be one more of us in a little while.'

Rosie had been excited and she couldn't get back to sleep. The midwife came and went into her mum and dad's room. There had been a bit of banging about and coming and going up the stairs, and once she thought she heard her mum cry out. Then, sure enough, when it was nearly morning, she heard a baby cry.

A baby's cry, from nowhere really. One minute no baby. The next minute, a baby. It was at that moment that she realised it was a real human being, come to share their lives.

After a while, her dad popped his head round the door again. 'Still awake, Rosie?' her dad had said. 'Come and see your new brother.'

She went slowly across the landing and into the room. Her mum was sitting up in bed with her hair looking sweaty, and – sure enough – she was holding a new baby. And, would you believe, it was feeding from her breast already.

'Isn't he a greedy thing?' her mum had said. 'No sooner out than on. Come and see, Rosie.'

So Rosie sat on the bed, feeling a bit awkward, and looked at the baby and at her mum and dad who had big silly grins on their faces.

The baby had been the centre of attention all week. Both grans and grandads had been fussing round. The neighbours had been in, and Auntie Sally. Everyone had spoken to Rosie of course, but she could tell that it was just so she didn't feel left out. Really, they had come to see the baby. They all stood round cooing at the baby, and Mum and Dad looked so proud and happy.

Rosie loved baby Jack, there was no doubt about that. He was her new brother and she was so proud of him. But at the same time she was just a bit – well, jealous really. She'd been the centre of attention up to now, and suddenly here was this baby taking up her mum and dad's time and being the star when the visitors came.

She lay in bed that night, a week after Jack was born, and looked around at her room. 'Will this always be my room?' she wondered. 'Or will I have to share it with Jack when he's too old to sleep with Mum and Dad?'

I love my new brother, but…

Just then, there was a footstep outside her door and her dad's head poked in. 'Are you awake, Rosie?' asked her dad. Then he came in and sat on the side of her bed.

'OK, Rosie?' her dad said. 'Been quite a week hasn't it? What do you think of your new brother?'

'I like him, Dad,' said Rosie. 'He's a lovely baby. I love him, I think.' But there was just something in her voice.

'But you just wonder what's going to happen now that he's here,' said Dad. 'That right?' Rosie nodded, and her dad went on.

Put up the OHT provided.

'We're bound to spend a lot of time with baby Jack, Rosie. He's very new. He can't feed himself, or walk, or do anything. We have to do everything for him. But we want you to remember that you are very special to us. You came first. Our lovely girl. We'll always love you very much, just so long as we are here. This is your home. This is your room. Nobody will take anything away from you. Soon you'll be able to help us to look after Jack, and we'll all go for walks together and in the park. We'll go on holidays together and there'll be four of us charging about in the woods and hearing Mum's stories by the fire at night. You see. Things are going to be even better now.'

Rosie nodded. Her dad kissed her and went out of the room. Rosie closed her eyes. Tomorrow morning she'd go in and have a look at Jack. He needed as much love as he could get, so that one day he could start giving some back. Soon he'd know how to smile at her. Now that would really be something.

✦ Conclusion

What Rosie was learning here was that love is something you give freely. She was also learning that love is not like the water in a bucket, or the rice in a bowl, that's gone when the bucket or the bowl are empty. The amount of love we have to give is always the same. If you give one person a lot of love, it doesn't mean that you have less for someone else. So if Rosie's mum and dad love their new baby, it doesn't mean that they have less love to give to Rosie. Their love for Rosie is just the same. She might have to share her parents' time with Jack, but she doesn't have to share their love. They can give all their love to Jack and they can also give all their love to Rosie. That's what love is like.

A prayer

Lord, you taught us the importance of love.
And you taught us that love is not always easy.
Help us to love and understand the people around us in our families and in our school.
Amen.

A thought

You don't share your love out. You give everybody all the love you have.

Song suggestions

'I will always be there,' *Primary Assembly Song Book* 40

'Praise to God for things we see,' *Someone's Singing Lord* 20

Optional follow up

Discuss – or make your own list of – all the changes that happen in a family when a new baby arrives.

Working away from home

Assembly 1 of 4

This offers reassurance that home and family exist even people are away from home. It tells of a girl whose dada works away from home all week. As the week goes on, she and her mum think about him, and he thinks about them.

You will need

- nothing at all.

Taken by ....

Date ....

Given to ....

Comments

- ....
- ....
- ....

✦ Introduction

I want you to pretend that you are in your house.

Someone is going out. Who might it be?

Take suggestions – mum or dad going shopping, grandad going to the allotment, brother going out to work, etc.

Let's wave goodbye to each of them.

Do this and after each wave say:

Is *(he/she)* coming back? Of course *(he/she)* is. Here *(she/he)* comes. Say hello!

Sometimes it's you who is going out. Where are you going?

Take suggestions – to school, out to play, to the shop, etc.

Let's wave goodbye as we go.

Do this and after each wave say:

Are you coming back? Of course you are. Here you come. Hello, I'm back!

When you're away, your home is still there isn't it?

Do you think about it? Think about it now. Think about the rooms, and your own room, and the people in the house, and the pets. There it is, safe and sound waiting for you to come home.

And it's like that for everyone who goes out. People like to get back don't they?

They say, 'It's good to be home!' and they flop down into a chair.

Even after a really great day out or a holiday, people say, 'It's good to be home!'

Today I'm going to read you a story about somebody who has to be away from home a lot.

But all the time he is away, his home is still there waiting, and when he comes home, his family makes him welcome.

Working away from home

Story

It was still dark outside Jenny's bedroom window, but something had woken her up. She knew what it was – her dad was getting up to go to work.

Jenny knew the routine. First Dad went into Mum with a cup of tea. There was a murmur of voices. Then he tiptoed into her own bedroom, trying not to wake her.

But of course she was already awake, and she grinned up at Dad as he bent over to give her a kiss.

'Bye, Jenny!' he said. 'You go back to sleep now. I'm just off.'

'Bye, Dad!' Jenny said and reached up for a hug.

Then Dad went quietly out of the room, pulling the door shut. She heard his footsteps on the stairs, then a quick bark as Dad rubbed Scamp's ears on the way out.

Then came the sound of the front door opening and shutting, and then the car door, and then the sound of the car starting up and reversing off the drive.

At that point she sat up, as she always did, and listened carefully as the car drove away, trying to hear it for as long as possible as it went off down the road in the quiet of the early morning.

Later, as she had breakfast with her mum, Jenny sighed. Mum knew what the sigh was all about.

'Monday morning again, eh Jenny!' said Mum. 'Dad off again and not back till Friday. It seems a long time doesn't it?'

Jenny nodded and played with her toast.

'He has to go away to work, you know that,' explained Mum.

Jenny looked sad and her mum hugged her and said, 'There's no work round here, and it's too far to travel to Birmingham every day, so he just has to spend all week there and see us at the weekends.'

Jenny looked across at Scamp, who lay by the fireplace with sad eyes looking up at her. She played with her toast a bit more and wondered where Dad was just now.

At that moment, Dad was just turning off the M6 at Spaghetti Junction, and starting down the expressway into Birmingham. He glanced at the car clock.

'Eight o'clock,' he said to himself. 'Jenny will be playing with her toast and wondering what I'm doing.'

He smiled and made a picture in his head of the scene round the breakfast table back at home.

At ten o'clock that day, Jenny was at school, reading quietly from her book and waiting for Mrs Meredew the classroom helper to come and hear her read.

Suddenly, she looked up at the clock and sat back for a while, wondering what her dad was doing and feeling just a little that she was missing him, even though there was lots to do at school.

What her dad really was doing at that moment was sitting back from his computer screen and stretching himself. He looked at the little clock in the corner of the screen – ten o'clock.

Working away from home

Then he looked out of the window, across the rooftops into the distance, as if he was trying to see all the way home and all the way to Jenny's classroom.

'Wonder what she's doing now?' he said to himself. 'Reading probably. I hope so, because she's really coming on with her reading.'

'Penny for your thoughts!' said the man opposite him.

Jenny's dad smiled and answered, 'Just thinking about the family. Wondering what they're up to.'

Sometimes he would look up from his computer screen and stare into space, and the man opposite would smile because he knew what he was thinking.

Sometimes he would stop in the middle of eating his lunch and sit quite still, and the ladies in the cafeteria would know what Jenny's dad was thinking.

Sometimes he would wake up in the night in his little flat and think about Jenny and Jenny's mum, curled up in the big bed together, and he would miss them very much.

The week went on. Jenny thought about her dad a lot. Sometimes she would go quiet when she was eating her breakfast or her tea, and her mum would know what she was thinking.

Sometimes she would look up from her work at school and stare at nothing in particular, and her teacher would know what she was thinking.

Sometimes she would wake up in the night and go and get in her mum's bed, because they were both missing Dad.

All week, Scamp moped about the house and kept looking expectantly at the front door.

'What you have to remember, Jenny,' said her mum one night as they lay in the big bed. 'Is that we're luckier than lots of people. At least your dad has a job, which a lot of people don't have. We have a home and enough to eat. We love each other very much and we'll always be here to make Dad welcome when he comes home on Fridays.'

As the week went on Jenny's dad thought about Jenny and her mum a lot.

In the end, though, Friday came round like it always did.

At school, Jenny was impatient for the day to finish, and she hurried home with her mum.

The evening went on and the darkness came, and they kept looking at the clock and then at the table laid for three people.

And on the M6, Jenny's dad fretted in the traffic jams and looked at the clock in the car and thought of home, the table laid for tea and Jenny and her mum sitting looking at the clock on the mantelpiece.

Soon, the traffic cleared and, before long, Jenny's dad was turning off the motorway and making his way through the streets to their home.

As he turned the corner at the end of their road, he pipped his horn and then revved up a bit as he turned onto the drive at the front of the house.

Long before he did that, though, Scamp had sat up with his ear pricked.

'Is it him, Scamp?' Jenny had asked and Scamp had trotted to the door.

At the same time, Jenny had heard the horn and the car turning on to the drive.

She ran to the door and opened it, just in time to see her dad locking the car up and turning to the house.

Scamp ran out and Dad bent down to rub his head and looked over him at Jenny.

'Hi Jen!' he called out. 'Here I am again!'

Jenny ran out, grinning all over her face, while her mum stood framed in the brightly lit doorway.

'The same smashing Friday scene,' said Jenny's dad to himself. 'Worth it in the end.'

✦ Conclusion

We all have to leave our homes to go to places – to work, to school or to go shopping – but our homes are there all the time we are away, and they will be there when we get back.

Even if someone has to leave home for a long time, they can come back and everyone will make them welcome. When that happens, it often helps them to know that their home and all the people in it will be there when they get back.

A prayer

Dear God, we thank you for our homes. We thank you for the love of our families. Protect people who are away from home and bring them back safely to their loved ones.

In particular, please protect those people who have no homes because of war. Keep them safe until the time comes when they can have homes once again. Amen.

A thought

Your home is still there even if you can't see it. And if you close your eyes and think about your family, then they can also close their eyes and think about you. And that's the next best thing to being together.

In a way, you are always together if you can think about each other and look forward to being really together.

Song suggestions

''Think on these things', *Someone's Singing Lord*, 38

'How many people live in your house?', *Tinder Box*, 19

Optional follow up

Ask the children to find out about how another member of their family spends their day and to write a diary or draw a picture to illustrate it.

Invite someone who works away from home to come in and talk about it – give them a copy of this assembly in preparation.

Four generations

The family photograph

Four generations

Assembly 2 of 4

This assembly uses the story of a family photograph to help children understand how family relationships are organised. It reinforces the concept from older members to newcomers.

You will need

- the OHT provided.

Taken by ....

Date ....

Given to ....

Comments

- ....
- ....
- ....

✦ Introduction

Who has had a new baby in the family lately?

Take any names of new babies.

Now, does anybody have a brother or sister who is much older than them? Has anybody's older sister or brother had a new baby? In other words, has anybody had a new nephew or niece?

Again take any names.

There's something special about that, isn't there?

It's a new generation – the next generation younger than yourself.

It reminds you that as time goes on, new generations of people keep arriving to keep the family going.

Let's hear a story about a family.

Story

It was Monday morning in Class 2 and Mrs Fuller was busy with all the usual things – the register, some notes from parents and the dinner money envelopes.

In the middle of it all, children were coming up to her with stories about the weekend.

'Miss! Our cat got lost on Saturday! But she came back the next day!'

'Miss! I've brought my birthday cards in to show!'

For now, while she was trying to concentrate on a lot of things at once, Mrs Fuller just kept nodding, smiling and saying, 'Oh yes?' and 'How nice for you!'

But Mrs Fuller had heard all of these bits of news and had stored them away in her mind so that she could ask about them again later when things settled down a bit.

In particular, she was determined to ask Justine what she had meant when she had called out, 'Miss, we had a special photograph

Four generations

taken with our new baby and my gran and everybody on it on Saturday.'

Mrs Fuller knew that Justine's older sister Anne-Louise had had a new baby just a week ago. Justine had been really excited about it.

Mrs Fuller also knew that it was quite a big family.

Later, Mrs Fuller called the class to sit on the carpet and she joined them on her low seat in the corner.

For a while various people told their stories.

Then Mrs Fuller said, 'Now Justine, tell us about this photograph!'

Justine took a deep breath and then said, 'Well, it was like this. My dad said that now we had a new baby, and my gran was still alive, there were four generations in our family.'

She held up her hand to count them off on her fingers.

'There's Gran Williams. There's my dad and Uncle Jim who are Gran Williams's sons. There's Anne-Louise and me. That's three generations. And now Anne-Louise has baby Joseph. That makes four. My dad said that lots of families don't manage to have all four generations alive at the same time.'

Mrs Fuller nodded. 'That's true, not every family is lucky enough to see it. Now, answer me this question. Who is baby Joseph's grandad?'

Justine knew straightaway, because she had realised it when the baby was born.

'My dad!' she said, smiling.

'That's right,' said Mrs Fuller. 'Your dad is also a grandad. Now tell me something else. What are you to baby Joseph? You're not his sister, because his mum is your sister. So what are you? You're the baby's...'

'Auntie!' said Justine. 'I'm Joseph's Auntie Justine!'

Mrs Fuller nodded and said, 'So Joseph is your... '

'Nephew!' said Justine quickly. She knew all this because she was very proud of it.

'Right!' said Mrs Fuller. 'One more question. What's the name of Anne-Louise's husband – Joseph's dad?'

'Tom,' said Justine.

'And Tom is your... '

'Brother-in-law!' said Justine triumphantly. She wasn't going to be caught out.

Mrs Fuller laughed. 'Carry on with the story now,' she said.

'Well,' said Justine. 'My dad said that we ought to have a family photograph while Gran's still well enough and while Joseph's small. My mum said we'd never get everybody together, and it was one of my dad's ideas that wouldn't work. But he spent ages sorting it out.'

Justine explained in great detail how her dad had phoned everyone up, booked the photographer and arranged for everyone to meet on the Saturday morning at their house.

'We had a house full,' she said to the class. 'Mum was in the kitchen making tea and coffee all morning and she kept grumbling at my dad.'

That made everybody laugh – they all knew the kind of thing Justine meant.

Justine was really into the story now and she continued, 'Mum kept saying, "I hope you're happy. All this was your idea. But you aren't having to do all the work are you?" and things like that.'

'Tell us some more,' called out Lee from the back of the class.

'Well, there was my cousin Terry,' said Justine. 'He's a real terror – like his name everyone says. He picked all my mum's best flowers from the garden and ended up completely covered in mud!'

Mrs Fuller tutted a bit.

Justine said, 'We all got tidied up for the photograph though. Not that Gran minded. She kept saying to Mum, "Leave the children alone, they're enjoying themselves." But Mum said she'd had enough nonsense.'

Then she added, 'Gran had a great time. She kept asking for more cups of tea and when she said to Mum, "Haven't you any chocolate biscuits?", Mum sort of made a face behind her back.'

'What was little Joseph doing among all of this?' asked Mrs Fuller. 'Sleeping, I expect.'

'Mostly,' answered Justine. 'But he woke up when we all went into the sitting room for the photograph.'

Then Justine described how Gran had sat in the middle. The grown ups had stood behind Gran.

Gran had held Joseph with Anne-Louise right next to her – her hand on Gran's shoulder. Next to Anne-Louise was Tom.

'Where were you?' asked Mrs Fuller.

'I stood at the side of Gran, on the other side to Anne-Louise, with my hand on Gran's shoulder too,' Justine said very seriously.

'You know, I bet that makes a lovely photograph,' said Mrs Fuller. 'When will you see it?' she added.

'The photographer's bringing a copy round tonight,' replied Justine proudly.

Then came questions from the rest of the class. And it was Lee again who wanted to know more.

'Was your mum happy in the end?' he asked Justine.

'Oh yes!' said Justine laughing. 'She grumbles, but it's never serious really. She gave Dad and me a big hug when it was all over and said, it was a lovely day but next time there was a family photograph could it be done at Uncle Jim's house please, and could somebody remember to get chocolate biscuits for Gran.'

 ISBN 1 874050 55 4

Four generations

✦ Conclusion

Let's see that picture shall we?

Put up the OHT provided.

Just think, a four-generation family photograph!

I wonder if anyone here has that many generations in their family.

It's a good idea to have a picture like this to remember everybody by. People far in the future will look at it. I expect that Justine's dad will write on the back when it was taken and who everyone in it is, so that no details are forgotten.

When Joseph looks at it, when he's grown up, he'll be able to remember all the people on the photograph, even if he can't remember the day it was taken.

A prayer

Lord, you taught us the importance of love. And you taught us that love is not always easy. Help us to love and understand the people around us in our families and in our school. Amen.

A thought

Generations come and go – as older people leave us, new babies join us. But life continues, with each of us passing on love from those who are older to those who are younger. We all have a part to play in this.

Song suggestions

'Family prayer', *Primary Assembly Song Book*, 85

'How many people live in your house?', *Tinder Box*, 19

Feeding the baby

Assembly 3 of 4

This assembly is about the special bond of love between a mother and her children, expressed in the way that she provides their food. There is a reassuring, gentle story about a mother breast-feeding her baby while her little son looks on.

You will need

- nothing at all.

Taken by ....

Date ....

Given to ....

Comments

- ....
- ....
- ....

✦ Introduction

In this assembly we are going to look at the importance of eating and drinking as a social occasion at home or in school and especially the importance of the love shown when a mother is feeding her baby.

Have you all had breakfast this morning? I hope so, because you need to get some energy at the start of the day.

Food is important to us right from the moment we are born. When a baby is born what's the first thing that he or she does? Can you tell me?

Take suggestions.

Yes, a baby cries – like a protest because he or she was somewhere warm and comfortable and is now in the big, wide world.

Usually the baby is hungry too and the mother will give him or her some milk. She might give some of her own milk that she's made in her body, just as other creatures do, or she might give some milk in a bottle. Either way she will cuddle her baby close to show her love.

The milk she gives is part of that love. In no time at all the baby is contented because he or she feels the mother's love.

The baby grows up and the people looking after him or her carry on showing their love by providing the child with food, warmth and clothing.

It continues to be like that – when you go from school to your home, or to your gran's house, or to someone who cares for you, then you will nearly always have something to eat, prepared for you by someone who loves you.

Let's hear a story about that.

📖 Reading

Michael quite liked the feeling of having a new sister. It did cause some upsets of course – little Sarah had a habit of waking up in the night and crying, and waking everyone up. She did take up a lot of everyone's time.

Sometimes Michael felt that his mum didn't have time to listen to him because she was looking after Sarah, but he understood that. His mum had been careful to explain before

Feeding the baby

Sarah arrived just how much time she would need.

'So, Michael,' his mum had said. 'If I spend a lot of time looking after the new baby, it doesn't mean I love you less. In fact I'll love you more, because the new baby will fill me with lots of love for everyone. And you'll be able to help with the baby.'

Michael was quite interested in that.

'Will I be able to give him his bottle?' he asked.

'For a start,' his mum said, 'it might not be a he. And for another thing, I hope to be feeding the baby myself.'

Michael understood the first thing – about the baby not necessarily being a he. But he was a little puzzled by the second thing, about his mum feeding the baby herself.

But soon after Sarah arrived – a she, not a he – he understood what his mum said about feeding the baby herself. Soon after his mum got home, he went into the bedroom to where his mum was resting on the bed.

'I'm going to feed Sarah now. Stay and see,' said Michael's mum.

Michael watched as his mum picked little Sarah out of her crib and held her close to her on one arm. With the other hand, she unbuttoned her blouse and Sarah started to suck hungrily on her mum's breast.

'How did she know how to do that?' asked Michael.

His mum smiled and said, 'Did you see how her head moved quickly as she was searching for my breast. That's called "rooting". All newborn babies do that. A little baby turns automatically towards anything that brushes her cheek. That's how she finds her food.'

'Did she know how to suck as well?' asked Michael.

'Oh yes,' answered his mum. 'She needed a little bit of encouragement at first. I just stroked her cheek a bit, but she soon got going. You see all small creatures are born knowing how to feed. They need to be able to do that.'

Michael thought for a bit. Then he asked, 'Did I do that? Did you feed me like that?'

His mum nodded. 'Yes and I remember it very well. You were so young then that you won't remember it.'

Michael thought perhaps that he did remember it. Somewhere, deep in his mind, was a thought that he recalled a special feeling of the warmth and comfort of his mum close to him.

His mum held her free arm out to him. He climbed up on the bed and snuggled up.

'Sing, Mum,' said Michael. So his mum quietly sang some of his favourite songs such as 'Lightly Row' and 'Puff the Magic Dragon'. Michael curled up against her.

'What's Sarah doing now?' he asked.

His mum looked down at her.

'Well, actually, she's gone to sleep. Perhaps she's had enough dinner now, but she can stay there a bit, just enjoying being close to us. Then she can go in her cot and we'll go down and have our dinner together.'

It was warm in the bedroom. Sarah was sleeping. Mum was still tired from when Sarah was born and from waking in the night to feed her, so she dozed, just half asleep.

Michael was awake, but he was content to lie quietly against his mum. He could feel her body moving as she breathed, and he could hear Sarah making little snuffling noises in her sleep. It was a good time and a good feeling. He yawned as he ran over his mum's songs again in his mind.

'I wonder what's for dinner?' he thought, and he hoped it would be spaghetti hoops.

✦ Conclusion

Love is shown in so many different ways. But when we see parents giving food to their children – when they are giving milk, or giving spoonfuls of dinner to a child in a high chair, or sharing a biscuit on the bus, then that reminds us of how much love there is in the family.

For baby Sarah, taking food was also taking love from her mother, and her brother Michael was able to share in that love, and to understand his love for his mother and for his sister.

A prayer

Dear God, we thank you for the food we eat. We thank you for the people in our families who provide it for us. When we were babies, they showed their love for us by looking after us, and feeding us, and we learned from them about loving and caring. Amen.

A thought

It's not enough for a mother just to love her baby. She has to feed and care for him or her as well. But the feeding and caring become part of that love.

Song suggestions

'How many people live in your house?',
Tinder Box, 19

'If I could be a bubble',
Primary Assembly Song Book, 81

 ISBN 1 874050 55 4

Gran on the Internet

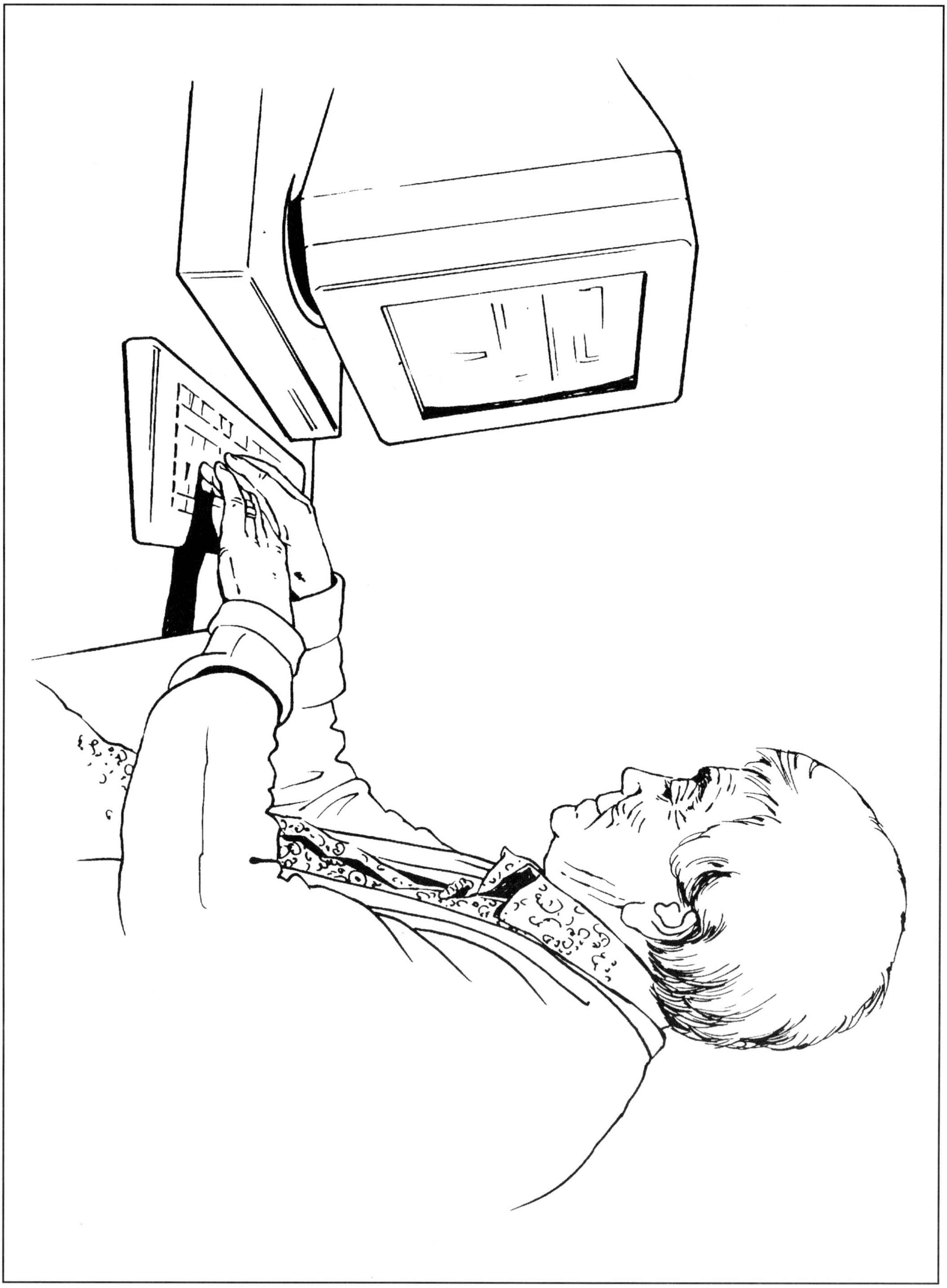

Gran on the Internet

Assembly 4 of 4

This assembly finds Gran in the retirement home. She makes some new friends, and learns how to use a computer to get on the Internet. It emphasises that age is no barrier to learning, and that older people are often filled with a zest for living.

You will need

- the OHT provided.

Taken by ....

Date ....

Given to ....

Comments

- ....
- ....
- ....

✦ Introduction

Who knows how to use a computer?

Yes, you all do. It's something we do every day here. You use them in class, and we use them in the offices. We don't think twice about it.

But sometimes older people find computers a bit off-putting. That's because they've grown up without them, and they think it might be difficult to learn about them. And in any case, they manage perfectly well without them, so they wonder if they really need to use them.

But of course, with computers, anyone, of any age, can do things that they couldn't do before. You can produce smart-looking letters and booklets, for example.

Most importantly, though, you can get on the Internet, and you can send emails. That will really add to the lives of people who can't get out and about much.

That's what Gran finds out in this story.

🕮 Story

It was Saturday morning, and Roberta was going with her Auntie Sylvia to see her gran in the retirement home.

'Is Gran really alright in the home?' asked Roberta.

Auntie Sylvia nodded. 'She seems OK now. She was a bit unhappy at first, especially because she couldn't bring many of her own things with her. But she's got to know a few people now, and we usually find her chatting to someone when we arrive – that's a good sign.'

When they got to the home, they went straight in. Auntie Sylvia smiled at one of the care workers on duty. 'Hi, Delice,' she said. 'Where's Mum today?'

Delice laughed. 'Oh, you wait and see. You'll find her in the little room off the main lounge. She's with Derek.'

They found the room, and went in. For a moment they stood there, taking in a surprising scene.

Gran on the Internet

'She's on the computer!' said Roberta.

Put up OHT provided.

Gran didn't turn round. 'Shush!' she said. 'I'm on the Internet.'

Sitting beside Gran was a young man – a boy really. He was leaning forward like people do when they are helping someone on the computer, but when he heard Sylvia and Roberta speak, he sat up and turned round.

'Hello,' he said, with a big smile.

'This is Derek,' said Gran, but she didn't turn round. 'Derek is from the High School. He's helping me with the computer.'

'It's part of a community project I'm doing at school,' said Derek.

'I didn't even know they had computers here,' said Auntie Sylvia.

'It's part of the same project,' said Derek. 'The school has persuaded one of its own sponsors to put three PCs in here.'

'Shush,' said Gran again. 'Now, Derek, love. Just tell me how to find my favourite sites again will you? I want to look at that one about *Ready, Steady Cook*. I liked that one.'

'Gran!' said Auntie Sylvia. 'Will you stop for a minute. We've come to visit you.'

Gran sighed and turned round in her chair. Derek said, 'I've got to go now, anyway. You know how to shut down the computer. Bye everybody.' And off he went.

'He's a good lad, that one,' said Gran. 'A real gem. He's got us all going on computers. He's going to help me to find some email pen pals next Wednesday.'

Auntie Sylvia shook her head in amazement. When she and Roberta were on their way home, Sylvia kept saying, 'Well, I never. Who'd have thought it?'

Roberta laughed. 'Are you surprised then, Auntie Sylvia?'

Auntie Sylvia laughed too. 'You can say that again. It's alright for you – you're growing up with computers and you probably don't see anything surprising in them. But Gran – well, there were only typewriters when she was at work. I don't know how she does it.'

The following Saturday, Roberta went again with her Auntie Sylvia. This time they found Gran sitting having a cup of tea with two of the other residents. Roberta and her auntie joined them.

'No computer today?' Auntie Sylvia asked.

Gran looked up. 'Oh, hello,' she said. 'No, Derek was here earlier today, and someone else is on them now. We'll have to get some more. In fact I'm thinking of getting my own. Derek knows a good place.'

Sylvia laughed. 'Mum, you never fail to surprise me,' she said.

Gran went on, and pointed to her friends at the table. 'I was just telling these two. I've been emailing a woman in Chicago. She's interested in the work I used to do at the hat factory, because she did the same sort of job. Fancy that. All that way away and she worked in a hat factory too.'

'Quite amazing,' said Sylvia, in a faint sort of voice.

'And,' said Gran, 'I've found an old friend! How about that?'

'How about it?' said Sylvia. 'Go on, surprise me some more. Was it Charlton Heston? He was always one of your favourite men.'

'No,' said Sylvia. 'But there's lots about him on the Web. No, Derek showed me how to use an email address finder, and I looked up Colin Drimthrope. He emigrated to New Zealand forty years ago, and I hadn't heard from him. But I found his email address, and we've been in touch three times.'

Roberta laughed. 'Can you just find anybody then?' she asked.

'Not really,' said Gran. 'I was lucky with Colin. He has an unusual name, and then, of course, it was lucky he was on email – though he was the sort of person who would be. He made his own radio set when we were still at school.'

On the way home, Roberta said. 'Gran seems quite happy, doesn't she?'

Auntie Sylvia nodded and said one of her favourite sentences again – 'You can say that again. She's found a new interest, made some new friends.'

'She might even have a visit from Charlton Heston!' suggested Roberta, and both she and Auntie Sylvia laughed and they walked cheerfully home hand in hand.

✦ Conclusion

When you think about it, two things have happened to Gran that are the opposite of each other, in a way.

She has gone into a retirement home, and that's made her life a bit more restricted. She's not in her own home, and she hasn't got all her own things with her. And she can't get out and about as much as she could before.

But at the same time, her life has also become less restricted. She's made new friends in the home, and that's broadened her horizons a bit, and she's learned a new skill with the computer, which will open out her life even more.

It's never too late to learn. Never too late to make new friends. Never too late to look further into the world.

A prayer

Lord, we thank you for the ability to make new friends, and to make contact with old friends. We thank you for computers that make more things possible. Help us to make sure that computers help our lives and don't get in the way of what we want to do. Amen.

A thought

You can get out and about in more ways than one these days. In a way, you can use a computer to travel the world without leaving your desk.

Song suggestions

'Keep on Going', *Primary Assembly Song Book*, 90

'Hands to work and feet to run', *Someone's Singing Lord*, 21

Marcus does the wheelie bin

Assembly 1 of 4

This assembly is about valuing people who do jobs that go unnoticed. It tells of Marcus, the singing bin man. Marcus realises that his work is important and that what he does is appreciated by others.

You will need

- some examples of rubbish, for example empty cartons and apple cores
- a blank OHT and pens.

Taken by ....

Date ....

Given to ....

Comments

- ....
- ....
- ....

✦ Introduction

Look at this rubbish.

Do you have rubbish in your house? I bet you do. I can't think of anyone who doesn't have some rubbish.

What things get thrown out in your house and end up in the bin outside?

Take suggestions and make a list on the OHT.

Well, that's an awful lot of rubbish.

Tell me, what happens to it after it goes in the bin?

That's right. The bin lorry comes round and the bin men and women pick up the bins and empty them into the lorry.

Do you think this is an easy job? Give me some reasons why it's not an easy job?

Take suggestions, for example the bins are heavy/smelly and can have dangerous things in them (broken glass or jagged cans), the weather can be bad and they have to work early in the morning.

Emptying the bins is important and the people who do it are helping us to live healthy and more pleasant lives. The bin lorry crews are people who help keep our community clean and today we will look at the work they do.

The teams who work on the bin lorries have a difficult job to do. There must be times when they find it difficult to keep cheerful.

This story is about Marcus, who did manage to keep cheerful most of the time.

🕮 Story

Marcus liked to sing while he was working.

He sang gospel songs mainly. 'People get ready, there's a train a-comin' was one of his favourites. 'Amen!' was another.

He would sing as the truck was going along and he would sing as he was picking up the bins from outside people's houses.

First the truck would stop in whichever road Marcus and his team were going to work in.

Marcus does the wheelie bin

Marcus and his workmate, Steve, would get out, and they would go to the bins which people had left by the roadside and bring them to the truck.

They would put them two at a time in a special lift at the back of the truck.

The lift would tip the bins into the back of the truck and then put the bins down again.

Marcus and Steve would then put the bins back in front of the houses where they belonged.

They had good days and bad days.

Let me tell you about one of Marcus's days that was a bit of both.

For a start, it was raining when Marcus got up at five o'clock. It was still very dark too, and it would not be light until eight o'clock.

Marcus stepped out into the street and shivered. It was cold and the rain was sheeting down into big puddles in the gutter.

Then Steve was late. Gareth and Marcus waited for him at the depot.

They weren't really annoyed, because they were all friends and they had all been late at one time or another.

Then they had trouble with some of the bins.

One of them, at one house, had been filled with something really heavy. Steve joked that it was full of lumps of concrete.

It took both of them to move it and they thought it might break the lift on the truck, but in the end it was alright.

Then there was a really smelly bin. And I mean REALLY smelly.

Marcus didn't know what it had in it.

'And I'm not going to look!' he said.

Before he handled it, he put his scarf round his nose and mouth and sang songs through it in a muffled voice.

'Mffff, praise Him, mffff, nnnnn.'

'Tell you what, Marcus,' called Steve, 'your singing sounds a lot better like that. I think you should wear your scarf round your mouth all the time, especially when you feel a song coming on.'

Then the worst thing of all happened.

Marcus was running back to one of the houses pulling a wheelie bin – hurrying to try to make up time – when he stumbled over the kerb and fell full length.

He fell heavily on the edge of the pavement and felt a sharp pain.

His two workmates rushed over to help him up, but he groaned and gasped, 'No! Leave me on the ground a moment! I think my ribs are broken.'

It was cold and wet in the gutter, where Marcus was lying. Steve and Gareth didn't know what to do for a moment, then someone else appeared.

It was the lady who lived in the house that Marcus was taking the bin back to.

'Oh dear!' she said. 'I was watching from the doorway. I always like to hear him singing. Now he's hurt himself with my bin. I feel terrible! What can I do?'

'Can you fetch something to keep the rain off him?' asked Steve.

Marcus does the wheelie bin

Then he added, 'Please ring for an ambulance first.'

The lady was back in no time, with a big raincoat.

They laid it over Marcus, who was groaning with pain.

'Singing a different song now, eh mate?' said Steve.

Marcus groaned even louder.

'Don't make me laugh!' he said. 'It hurts me more when I laugh.'

The lady shook her head and smiled, 'He's a cheerful lad, isn't he? I watch him every week and it cheers me up to see him working and enjoying it. I hope he'll be OK. I rang the ambulance by the way.'

In no time, the ambulance came and took Marcus off to hospital.

Later that day, when they had finished work, Steve and Gareth went to visit him.

They found him sitting up in bed with his chest bandaged. He had a set of headphones on and a newspaper on his lap.

He was singing quietly to himself, but he took the headphones off when he saw his friends coming.

'Still singing, Marcus!' said Steve. 'I thought breaking your ribs might shut you up!'

'No,' said Marcus. 'I'm still praising the Lord in song.'

'Why?' asked Gareth. 'After the day you've had – the rain, having to hurry and smelly bins, and then this accident! What have you got to be thankful for?'

'Well, I'll tell you,' said Marcus. 'First off, my bones will get better. I'll be as good as new. Second, I had my good friends with me when I had my accident. You looked after me real well. Best of all, though, I had a visitor before you.'

Gareth and Steve looked at each other.

'Who was that?' they asked.

'The lady from the house where I fell,' Marcus answered. 'She brought me a big box of chocolates and she talked to me about how cheerful my singing made her feel, especially on dull mornings. She left me a card. There it is.'

He nodded to the card on his bedside table.

Steve picked it up.

'Read what she's written,' said Marcus.

So Steve read it aloud.

'For Marcus, the singing wheelie bin man. When I'm down, you cheer me up. When you're down, remember that without you and your mates we would be in real trouble. Keep doing a good job and keep praising the Lord.'

'There you are!' said Marcus. 'Somebody appreciates us.'

'Oh yes,' said Steve. 'But you know what worries me?'

'What's that?' asked Marcus.

Steve sighed. 'She's just encouraging you to do more singing. I'd like to find somebody who'll tell you to shut up.'

The three friends laughed. Marcus tried to lean out of bed to whack Steve with his newspaper, but the pain stopped him and he groaned, which only made Steve and Gareth laugh even more.

Marcus does the wheelie bin

✦ Conclusion

The lady's card said, 'Remember that without you and your mates we would be in real trouble.'

Why do you think the lady wrote that in her card?

Because without somebody to take away our rubbish, we would just have bigger and bigger piles of rubbish, and our lives would be impossible.

Picking up rubbish, and emptying bins, are not pleasant jobs, but we all depend on them being done.

The people who do jobs like that are important to all of us and it did Marcus and his friends good to be reminded of it, especially on a day when lots of things had gone wrong.

Does anyone pick up bins and rubbish at your house? Of course they do. They do at school here too.

Perhaps we hardly notice them. Perhaps we ought to appreciate them more.

Marcus praised God as he worked, because he believed that all work, honestly done, is a kind of worship – an opportunity to help other people and so to do something that God wants done.

A prayer

Dear God, we remember today all people who do unpleasant jobs on our behalf – clearing up rubbish, dealing with waste, working in all sort of weather and in all sorts of unpleasant conditions. Help us to appreciate the work that they do and to notice them as we pass by. Amen.

A thought

Not all jobs that have to be done are easy or pleasant. But if the people who do the unpleasant jobs are appreciated by everyone else, then perhaps the work becomes a little easier.

Song suggestions

'How we treat each other', Primary Assembly Song Book, 66

'Milk bottle tops and paper bags', Someone's Singing Lord, 17

Optional follow up

Write letters of appreciation to those who help around school and in the community.

Questions about school

Will the teachers and the other adults be kind to me?
Will I be able to do the work?
Will I have some friends?
Will someone help me if I don't know what to do?

When I first came to my school, I had things on my mind.
Would the work be hard or easy? Would the people here be kind?
When I first came to my school, there were things I longed to know
Who would be my teacher and where would I have to go?

Now I'm at my school, I feel better in my mind.
The work is hard and easy, but the adults here are kind.
I'm finding out the answers to the things I want to know
I know who is my teacher and where I have to go.

Now when I get home at night, my family say to me
'How much did you learn today? Can you count from one to three?'
I tell them I have learned much harder things today
I know some really useful words like 'dinner time' and 'play'.

So when I leave my school, and I've done with all this fuss
When I'm president of Cornwall or the boss of Toys R Us
Then I'll search into my mind and try hard to recall
The things that once I learned here, and I know I'll use them all.

Questions about school

Assembly 2 of 4

This assembly starts by asking some questions about your school – facts and figures – and moves on to the more fundamental aspects of the school community.

You will need

- a blank OHT and a pen
- the OHT provided.

Taken by ....

Date ....

Given to ....

Comments

- ....
- ....
- ....

✦ Introduction

In this assembly we're going to think about our own school and what it means to us. We come here every day, after all, and school is important in our lives. There is so much to think about – the people who work in school, the pupils, and all the learning that goes on. We will start today with some facts and figures.

I bet there are lots of things about our school that you don't know. There are certainly some things that I don't know.

Let's start by thinking of some questions about our school.

Where is it? What is the address?

How many children are here?

How many teachers and other adults are here?

How many classes are here?

When was the school built?

What's the headteacher's name?

Can we write in the answers to those on the OHP? Can you help me?

Take suggestions and write them on the OHT.

There are some questions that are a lot more important than that.

If you were a new pupil, coming here for the first time. What would you want to know?

I think I would want to know things like the questions at the start of this poem.

🕮 Poem

Put up the OHT provided and read the first verse.

Will the teachers and the other adults be
  kind to me?
Will I be able to do the work?
Will I have some friends?
Will someone help me if I don't know
  what to do?

The other things are useful to know, but these are the things that you really need to know. If the answer is yes to these things, then you know that you will be happy in school.

Questions about school

Continue reading the poem as follows.

When I first came to my school, I had things
on my mind.
Would the work be hard or easy?
Would the people here be kind?
When I first came to my school, there were
things I longed to know
Who would be my teacher and where would
I have to go?

Now I'm at my school, I feel better in my
mind.
The work is hard and easy, but the adults
here are kind.
I'm finding out the answers to the things
I want to know
I know who is my teacher and where I have
to go.

Now when I get home at night, my family
say to me
'How much did you learn today? Can you
count from one to three?'
I tell them I have learned much harder
things today
I know some really useful words like 'dinner
time' and 'play'.

So when I leave my school, and I've done
with all this fuss
When I'm president of Cornwall or the boss
of Toys R Us
Then I'll search into my mind and try hard
to recall
The things that once I learned here, and
I know I'll use them all.

In years to come, it will probably be the people who helped you who you remember – not just the teachers and the other adults, but the pupils who helped you to find things or helped you when you weren't sure what to do. Let's think about some of those and say thank you.

✦ Conclusion

Optional

This can easily be personalised, with names, and it can be made into a prayer, with 'Thank you Lord' as a response.

Thank you for the friend who helps me when I lose something.

Thank you for the teacher who helps me when I am stuck at something in my work.

Thank you for the person who helps me across the road.

Thank you for the person who looks after me on the playground.

Thank you for the person who looks after me at dinner time.

Thank you for the people who make the school warm and clean.

Thank you for the friend who makes me laugh.

Thank you for the friend who comforts me when I cry.

As we go through life, we will remember all of these people. Make sure that people will also remember you for the helpful things you have done.

A prayer

Dear God, we thank you for our school, for all the interesting facts and figures. But we thank you most of all for the people here and for the times when they are good to each other. Help us always to remember the people who treat us well and to keep them in our thoughts and memories. Amen.

A thought

As we go through life, we learn what things are important. We realise that kind acts are more important than simple answers and facts and figures.

Song suggestions

'Praise to God for things we see', *Someone's Singing Lord*, 20

'The what if song', *Primary Assembly Song Book*, 74

Optional follow up

- Conduct a survey on what people find most important about school.
- Ask the children to write letters of advice to someone starting at your school.

The little Dutch boy

Assembly 3 of 4

This assembly tells a version of the story of the Dutch boy who saved his community by stopping up a hole in the sea wall.

You will need

- nothing at all.

Taken by ....

Date ....

Given to ....

Comments

- ....
- ....
- ....

✦ Introduction

In our assembly today I'm going to tell you about a little boy who did a very brave thing for his village. We will think about our own actions and the effect they have on our own community.

Who's had something go wrong suddenly in the house? I know somebody who found a crack in a wall of their house. One day it wasn't there. The next day it was. The day after that it was a bit bigger. My friend had to do something quickly. It was no good sitting and thinking about it, or finding a book about cracks in the library. He had to get a builder in straightaway to mend it.

Some problems are like that – if you don't solve them straightaway they get worse, until they are just too big to solve at all.

The little boy in our story today knew that – he saw a problem and he did what he could to solve it quickly.

First, let me ask you if you know what a flood is? You might even have seen one. It's when a river, or the sea, spreads out over the surrounding land and the water gets into people's houses. Sometimes it's just very annoying, sometimes it's very serious.

In some places by the sea where there are big walls to keep the sea back, people have to be very watchful that the sea does not break down the sea wall or make a hole in it. In the Netherlands, a country not far away, there are lots of places by the sea that are protected by walls of stone or of earth. The people there are always careful to make sure that the sea walls – they call them dykes – are well looked after.

In the Netherlands there is a story that everyone knows, of a little boy who saved his village from flooding because he put his finger into a hole in the dyke and stopped the water from coming through. He knew that if the hole wasn't plugged while it was very small, it would get bigger and bigger so that nobody would be able to stop the water.

This story is based on that legend.

Story

Peter was standing at the back door of his family's small cottage, looking out at the stormy weather. The wind was blowing, and the rain was falling. 'What a terrible night!' said Peter. 'I keep thinking of the sea on the other side of the big dyke.'

His mother put her arm around him. 'I know, Peter,' she said. 'None of us like the wind and the rain, and we all know how close the sea is on the other side of the dyke. But we will be safe here in our house.'

All the people in the village where Peter lived knew about the sea. Long ago, the people who built the village had constructed a great dyke – a bank of earth and stone – to keep the sea out. They had built the dyke and then they had built their houses behind it, safe from the sea.

All the children were brought up to know how important their dyke was. If there was a weak spot in it and water leaked through, it could be very serious. If it were not stopped, the dyke would collapse and the sea would rush in and the village would be flooded.

Later that evening, after Peter and his mother had finished their supper, Peter's mother said, 'Oh, Peter, we are silly, we have forgotten your Gran's eggs!'

Every week, Peter or his mother took a basket of eggs from their chickens to Peter's grandmother.

'She'll be disappointed if she doesn't get them,' said Peter's mother. 'But I don't like to ask you to go there in this storm.'

'Don't worry mother,' said Peter. I'll be alright. Let me go. I like to go to Gran's house. She might give me some of her special cake.'

'Very well,' said Peter's mother. 'But you must stay and sleep in Gran's spare bed and come back to me tomorrow morning. That way you will only have one journey in the rain and the wind and the dark.'

So Peter set off to his grandmother's house, wrapped up against the wind and the storm, and carrying a basket of eggs for his grandmother.

The journey took him along the foot of the great dyke. Peter hurried along, thinking of the sea just on the other side of the bank. Then, suddenly, he stopped. He had walked into a puddle – no, not just a puddle from the rain. More like a little stream. Where could it have come from?

He stood and looked up at the dyke. The water was coming down the side of it. He scrambled a little way up the steep bank, following the stream of water. Then, in the darkness, he came upon what everyone in the village dreaded – a hole in the dyke!

In the dark it looked and felt like a small mouse hole, with a strong trickle of water coming out. Even as he looked, Peter saw earth and stones moving around the edge of the hole, and he knew that it would quickly get bigger.

'The hole is getting bigger all the time,' he thought. 'There is no time to get help. This is something I have to do now, straightaway. I must stay here and stop the water myself.'

So that is what Peter did. And what did he use? He used his own hand. He pushed it into the hole and clenched his fist so that it blocked the hole that the water was coming through.

The little Dutch boy

'I wonder how long I'll have to stay here,' he thought. 'Mum thinks I'm staying with Gran. Gran doesn't even know that I'm coming. And the weather is so bad that nobody will be out walking along the path by the dyke. No matter. I must stay and block the hole until someone comes.'

So that's what Peter did. Every few minutes he called out, 'Can anyone hear me? It's Peter, blocking a hole in the dyke! Here I am. Can anyone hear me?'

But the wind was fierce, and the rain was driving down, and nobody was out walking, so nobody could hear him. 'No matter,' thought Peter. 'I'll stay here all night if necessary. Then someone will find me in the morning when daylight comes.'

So that's what Peter did. His arm grew numb and he could no longer feel his hand. As the night drew on he drifted in and out of a dreamy sleep, then he would jerk awake and again he would call, in a weak voice, 'Can anyone hear me? It's Peter, blocking a hole in the dyke! Here I am. Can anyone hear me?'

The next morning, Matilde, one of the women from the village, was opening her curtains to see whether the rain had stopped when she spotted something. 'See, Michael,' she said to her husband. 'What is that on the dyke?'

Michael came to the window. 'It's... It's a man! No! It's a boy!'

And he ran out of the house, pulling on his heavy coat and shouting, 'Come everyone! There's a boy lying on the dyke!'

The people of the village ran to the dyke and found Peter. For a moment they stood looking up. 'He is surely dead!' they said, and then Peter raised his head and cried, 'Can anyone hear me? It's Peter, blocking a hole in the dyke! Here I am. Can anyone hear me?'

'He's blocking a hole in the dyke!' everyone cried. 'With his arm! He has surely saved us all!'

People quickly scrambled up the dyke to Peter. Some gently lifted him down while others set to work to repair the hole. 'Come Peter,' said Michael. 'It's time for a brave boy to go home.'

And they carried Peter to his house, to his astonished mother who thought he had been fast asleep in his grandmother's spare bed all through the night.

Peter recovered quickly, thanks to his mother's love and good cooking, and the day came when he stood before all the townspeople and was given a medal. 'To brave Peter,' it said on the medal. 'The boy who thought quickly and saved our village on the night of the great storm.'

✦ Conclusion

Did this really happen? Perhaps it did, but in any case there have been many examples of bravery of this kind. So the story stands for all acts of bravery – it is a symbolic story, of selfless action by a child who knew what to do.

The story tells us that if you see something wrong, or even if you do something wrong, then it's best to act quickly before it gets any worse. Here are some examples – see if you can think of some others.

If you fall out with a friend, make it up quickly before it becomes a real quarrel.

If you break something at home, don't hide it. Tell someone straightaway.

If someone is bullying you, tell your teacher or another adult straightaway, before it gets worse.

If you know your friend is doing something dangerous, tell someone before your friend gets hurt.

If you find something wrong in the cloakroom or an empty classroom, let someone know before it becomes a real problem.

Jesus often wanted quick decisions, because he knew he had an important task to do. He asked his followers to stop what they were doing and come with him. When people asked for help, he went straightaway to see what he could do. He knew perfectly well that if you want something to happen, then you have to do something about it.

A prayer

Lord, give us the strength and presence of mind to do what is right. Help us to plug the holes in our lives and our relationships before they become too big to be mended. Amen.

A thought

It's easy to forget things that we don't want to do. We tuck them away at the back of our minds, in the hope that they will go away. But if we bring them to the front of our minds, and deal with them, then they really will go away.

Song suggestions

'I did it!', *Primary Assembly Song Book*, 87

'For all the strength we have', *Someone's Singing Lord*, 16

Optional follow up

Much of Holland is made up of reclaimed land. See if you can identify it on a map, where it is usually called the Netherlands – if possible compare a modern map with one in an older school atlas. What happened to the Zuyder Zee?

Joining in

Assembly 4 of 4

This assembly is about sharing and joining in – an important skill reinforced during the early years of schooling. It tells of a small boy who, at first, finds it difficult to be with other children. His teacher and his classmates help him to find new enjoyment in his time at school.

You will need

- nothing at all.

Taken by ....

Date ....

Given to ....

Comments

- ....
- ....
- ....

✦ Introduction

In our assembly today we're going to hear about how we can work together and learn to accept one another for what we are. It can be difficult to do that, as Gordon and his classmates find in our story today.

In class we have to learn to work together, though it isn't always easy. Sometimes you have to stop doing what you want to do and do something else instead. You might be busy making something with a construction kit and teacher says, 'Everybody come and sit on the carpet,' or you might be interested in a book when the teacher says, 'Put your books away and look this way.'

Sometimes you have to work with other people in a group when you'd rather work on your own. Remember, though, that it's like that for other people in the class, too. They have to work with you when perhaps they would rather be doing something else.

It can be difficult to learn how to do this. Sometimes, it's especially difficult for anyone who spends a lot of time on their own at home, with no friends or brothers and sisters of the same age. Gordon was like that. He lived happily on a farm, hardly seeing any other children. When he started school it took him a bit of time to settle down. Here's Gordon's story.

🕮 Story

Gordon lived on a farm. He had the kind of life that you sometimes see in story books. In the early morning he helped his dad to milk the cows. Then he had his breakfast in the big farmhouse, at the table with his mum and dad and his older sister Maxine.

After breakfast, Maxine would go off to catch the bus to her big junior school in the next village, and Gordon would play by himself for a while, or he would go with his mum or dad to feed the chickens.

His favourite thing on the farm was the big tractor that his dad drove. Gordon knew all about it. Sometimes he sat up in the driving seat with his dad, and his dad explained the controls to him. Gordon would find pictures of tractors in his dad's magazines, and he had models of tractors in his toy box. He was tractor mad!

The time came, however, for Gordon to go to school. The nursery and infants school was in the village, a couple of miles away – first down a farm track and then a short distance along the lane.

First he went for a visit – his mum took him in the Land Rover and stayed with him. He played in the sandpit for a while and looked at the books around the room. He sat on the carpet and listened as the other children sang a song. On the whole, though, he didn't like it very much, and he was glad when his mum took him home and he could go out and see the chickens and the calves again.

'You know, Gordon,' said his mum when they had tea that day. 'Soon you will have to stay at school by yourself and I won't stay with you. But I will come back for you!'

Gordon thought about that for a while. He didn't think it was a good idea, but he didn't say anything. He just looked at his mum and carried on eating his tea.

So it was that, after a week or so of staying with Gordon, his mum one morning settled him down in the classroom and then said, 'I'm just going off to do a bit of shopping, and I'll be back for you in a while.'

In fact, she didn't really have to do any shopping, but all the same she left the Land Rover at school and walked the length of the village to Mrs Morton's shop, where she spent an hour talking to Mrs Morton.

Back at school, Gordon played with a toy fire engine for a while on his own. Mrs Fulton, his teacher, watched him. Then she said, 'Come along everyone, we're going to sit on the carpet and have a story now.'

The other children sat on the carpet to listen to Mrs Fulton, but Gordon just carried on playing with the fire engine.

'Come on, Gordon,' said Mrs Fulton. 'Come and sit with the others on the carpet and listen to the story.'

But Gordon shook his head. He wasn't really playing with the fire engine any more. He was just turning it around in his hands and looking down. Mrs Fulton looked at him, and she could see that he had tears in his eyes.

'Come on, Gordon,' she said. 'It's OK, we're going to have a nice story.'

But Gordon shook his head. 'I want my mum,' he said. 'When's my mum coming?'

'She'll be here soon,' said Mrs Fulton. But Gordon just stood by the table with the fire engine, crying quietly to himself and not letting anyone comfort him.

Mrs Fulton read a story to the rest of the group, but she kept an eye on Gordon, and the other children in the class kept looking round at him.

When Gordon's mum came he was still crying. He didn't run to her though. Part of him felt a bit let down really – his mum had never left him before. She picked him up and gave him a hug, and he soon felt better.

Joining in

The next day, there was a bit of a problem with the fire engine. When his mum left him, Gordon went across to play with it, but one of the other boys was already playing with it.

Gordon reached across and tried to take it off him. The other boy shouted, 'No! No!' and Mrs Fulton came across to see what was going on.

'Now then, Gordon! Jason! What's all this?' she said. Both boys were upset, and Jason said. 'Gordon tried to take the fire engine off me.'

Mrs Fulton kneeled down in front of the boys. 'Gordon, when someone's already playing with something, you can't just take it off them. It's not fair. We have to learn to share here, and let other people have turns with things.'

Gordon cried again at that, and went off on his own to sit in the corner. Again, he wouldn't come to sit with the others on the carpet.

Mrs Fulton was troubled, the other children were upset, and Gordon's mum was upset when she came to fetch him at the end.

Mrs Fulton said to Gordon's mum. 'It'll be alright – really it will. He's just not used to being with groups of other children. Bring him a few minutes later tomorrow and I'll have a word with the children first.'

Next morning, Mrs Fulton said to the other children, 'You know that we all have to learn how to share, and how to get on with each other. And you're all good at that. Well, we have to help Gordon enjoy being with us. So be patient with him, and kind. And show him that he can really have a good time here.'

But she did more than that. She knew what Gordon was interested in and what he knew about. So the next day, instead of a fire engine, Mrs Fulton put a model tractor on the table at the side of the room. Gordon started to play with it, and Mrs Fulton said, 'Do you like tractors, Gordon?'

Gordon nodded, and when it was time to sit on the carpet, she called him to come to the front holding the tractor. She stood him by her, and said to the other children, 'Today we're going to have a story about a tractor. But first, we'll ask Gordon to help us, because he knows all about tractors. I'll ask him some questions, and then you can ask him some too.'

And that's what happened. The children were really impressed by all the things that Gordon knew, and Gordon felt really proud. When he had finished answering questions, the other children clapped him.

'Well done, Gordon,' said Mrs Fulton. 'Now sit down on the carpet with the others and I'll read everyone a story about a tractor.'

And Gordon sat down with the other children without any fuss at all.

Gordon smiled and watched Mrs Fulton's face as she told her story. Then, when it was finished, she taught the class a new song about a tractor.

'I'm a big red tractor and I live in the yard.
I pull things and I drag things and I work extremely hard.'

Gordon liked the song, and soon he was singing it with the others.

When his mum came, Gordon had a big smile on his face, for the first time. On the way home in the Land Rover, he sang the tractor song, and his mum said a little prayer of thankfulness that Gordon was starting to enjoy his time in class. She was especially thankful for Mrs Fulton, and the other kind children in her class.

✦ Conclusion

Gordon settled down in his class. It took him a bit of time, because life at school was different from what he had been used to. What he needed was to find something he was good at – something that the other children would be interested in. Luckily his teacher was able to help him, and the other children were kind and understanding, and they helped him to join in and start enjoying his school days.

A prayer

Lord, help us all to be kind to new people who we meet or who come to join us in school. Help us to understand that they may feel lonely. Help us to find ways of including them in the things we do and the good times we have together. Amen.

A thought

When you reach out your hand, it can do one of two things. You can either reach out to push someone away, or you can reach out to draw them towards you. Which is best do you think?

Song suggestions

'The what if song', *Primary Assembly Song Book*, 74

'Look out for loneliness', *Someone's Singing Lord*, 36

Optional follow up

Talk about being lonely – discuss the feelings, and how it's possible to help people to overcome loneliness.

Doors

Doors

Assembly 1 of 4

This assembly is about the different signs you see on doors. It links this to the idea of a door as a way into something good. This in turn can link to the Christian message of Christ as the door to knowledge of God

You will need

- ***Optional*** prepare some cards with words found on doors, eg. Gents, Ladies, Entrance, Exit, etc.
- the OHT provided.

Taken by ....

Date ....

Given to ....

Comments

- ....
- ....
- ....

✦ Activity

If you have prepared cards, hold them up and ask the children to say the words. Alternatively, ask them to read the words as you write them on the OHT. Discuss the meaning of each one. Ask for more examples, especially of labelled doors in school.

A door is a way into something or a way out of something. It can be a bit of a mystery. Are there any doors in school that are a bit of a mystery to you? There are some places you're not allowed to go into *(give some examples if you can)*. Do you wonder what it's like in there?

Can you think of any doors in school that you really like to go through? There's the door you go through at the end of the day to meet your mum or dad or whoever is meeting you. There's the door into the dinner hall. Any more?

Who'll come out and be a door? *Choose a child.*

Now *(name)* you're a door. This side of you is inside. That side of you is outside. Here I come up the street. I'll knock on the door and see if anyone answers. There's no one to answer. Who'll come and answer the door? *Choose a child.*

Stand inside and get ready to answer the door.

Now, here I come up the street. I'll knock on the door and see if anyone answers.

The child says, 'Who's there?' Prompt if necessary.

It's only me. Can I come in?

The child replies, 'Yes.'

I'll open the door. My word it creaks. *(Tell the door to creak loudly.)* My word it creaks a lot. I'll open and shut it a few times. My word it does creak, doesn't it?

What does it need on the hinges?

'Oil.'

Yes, it needs some oil on the hinges. I need an oil can. Who'll come and be an oil can?

Choose a child.

I'll oil the hinges with my lovely big oil can. Thank you, oil can, you can sit down over here for a bit.

Doors

Now, I'm coming down the street. I'll knock on the door and see if anyone is there.

It's only me. Can I come in?

The child replies,'Yes.'

I'll open the door. It opens really quietly now. See? I'll open and shut it a few times and it really makes no sound at all. Hello, I'm the postman *(or woman)*. I've got a letter for you, but there's no letterbox in your door. Shall we make a letterbox in your door?

Help the door to make a letterbox with his/her fingers stuck out like scissors.

What a lovely letterbox. Who'd like to come and put things through the door? If you can think of something that comes through the door, then you can come and put it through.

Ask the pupils for examples. These might include: newspapers, letters, leaflets, notes...

Go through this little ritual every time with the pupils joining in:

Knock, knock, knock, here's something through your door.

Something through your letterbox and landing on the floor.

It's a – newspaper!

Now here's a door story.

📖 Story

Jim looked at his front door. It was really shabby. The paint was peeling off. The woodwork was going rotten. The letterbox was rusty. The number on the door was all crooked. 'I'll have to get a new door,' he thought. 'My door is important to me: I like visitors and I need visitors. I want them to see something good when they come to my house. If I have a shabby door, they might think I'm shabby myself. But where can I get one from?'

Jim went to his next-door neighbour, Mollie. 'Mollie, I need a new door. Have you got a spare one?' he asked.

'No, I haven't. I only have enough doors for myself. I have the same number of doors as I have doorways. No spares,' Mollie replied.

Jim came home and had a think. Nobody would have a spare door. Everyone would have the same number of doors as they had doorways. And he couldn't afford to buy a new one from the do-it-yourself shop. And although he had a workbench and could do repairs, he wasn't good enough at woodwork to make one for himself.

He went down to the cafe. He had a word with Big Bill, who worked behind the counter frying hamburgers and bacon. 'Hi, Big Bill. I've got this problem. I need a new door.'

'Well, don't look at me. I haven't got one. Tell you what though, I know someone who has,' Big Bill replied.

'Who?' Jim asked eagerly.

'The men who are knocking down the houses in Gordon Street. There are lots of doors there,' said Big Bill.

Jim went down to Gordon Street. The road was rough, and it wasn't easy to get down the street. The houses were being knocked down to make way for a new road across the town. There was smoke from fires, and piles of bricks. Jim had a good look round, though it was a bit of a struggle to get about, and soon he found a pile of doors. Some of them were in bad shape, like his own, but some were really good – almost new in fact. Jim found the foreman. 'I'd like one of those doors if I can,' Jim said.

'Right. You can have one for ten pounds,' answered the foreman.

'I've only got three,' Jim said.

The foreman looked at him. 'Oh, alright then,' he said.

'Can you give me a hand? I think I can get it home myself, if you've got some bits of rope,' Jim said.

The foreman got some rope, and managed to fasten the door to the back of Jim's wheelchair.

Jim set off back home. The wheelchair felt a bit unbalanced with the door fastened on the back, and he had to be careful not to knock any parked cars as he went along. There wasn't much room on the pavement and people kept stepping back to make room for him and making comments. 'What on earth have you got there, Jim? Are you moving house?'

Once, Jim caught the door against a lamp-post and came to a sudden halt that nearly threw him out of the chair, but he soon got going again.

When he got home, Mollie came out and unloaded the door from the wheelchair. 'I hope this door is going to fit your house, Jim,' she said. 'Let's try it,' Jim replied.

Jim went in and got a screwdriver, and together they took the old door off. The new door fitted nearly perfectly. It just needed a bit of planing off the bottom, and Jim did that in no time at his workbench in the shed.

When the door was fitted, Jim invited Mollie in for a cup of tea. 'You can be the first guest through my shiny new door. Perhaps I'll get more visitors now.'

'We know we're always welcome here, Jim,' said Mollie. 'Now you've got a happy door on a happy house.'

✦ Conclusion

Jim's door was important to him, because he wanted to welcome people into his home. The door is what you see when you visit somebody. It ought to welcome you.

Doors are important to us. A door can be open in welcome, or closed so that we are shut out. We can be like that – we can welcome people as friends, or shut them out.

When Jesus talked to his followers, he said, 'I am the Door'. He meant that if people followed him they would learn to know and understand more about God.

A prayer

Dear God, we go through doors all the time. Some of them we like, some of them we don't like very much. Help us to face whatever is on the other side with courage. And help us to be welcoming to others, to keep the doors of our hearts in good condition. Amen.

A thought

How many doors do we go through in a day? Can we work it out? How many doors will we go through in our lives? What surprises will we find? What good things and what not so good things? There are many adventures ahead.

Song suggestions

'The journey of life', *Someone's Singing Lord*, 28

'A house is a house for me', *Tinder Box*, 13

'The building song', *Come and Praise*, 61

Changing seasons

Assembly 2 of 4

This assembly reminds pupils that the seasons in this country may be less recognisable in other parts of the world or may happen at different times. It stresses that our seasonal and climatic changes in are part of the, world-wide system.

You will need

- a globe, autumn leaves, sunglasses, a scarf, a candle and matches and three large sheets of white paper

Taken by ....

Date ....

Given to ....

Comments

- ....
- ....
- ....

✦ Introduction

In this assembly, we are going to think about the changing seasons of the year and the enjoyment we get from each season as it comes round.

Hold up the globe and turn it slowly.

Here's our planet.

The Earth turns and all the time its surface moves from darkness to light and back to darkness as day follows night and night follows day.

Now walk the globe around in a big circle to indicate its movement around the sun, with the axis tilted.

The Earth moves around the sun.

As it does, the seasons of the year change.

Sometimes a part of the Earth will be under the direct rays of the sun. Other parts will take the sun's rays at an angle and the days will be shorter and the weather colder.

When it's summer in one country, it may be winter in another. When it is autumn in Europe, it will be spring in the South Pacific.

So, as we think today about our autumn and the falling leaves, let's remember how different it is in other countries right now.

The amazing way that our planet moves that gives us our autumn is also giving other parts of the world different seasons at exactly the same time.

We are all part of one planet. The winds that blow on us are part of huge world-wide changes.

Today we are going to celebrate the turning of the year and the turning of the Earth as our part of the planet moves from the long days of summer to the short days of winter.

It is a time when, for us, the ground begins to rest after growth and harvest.

Nature seems to sleep for a while, regaining its strength.

It is a sad time in many ways – a time for remembering warmth, sunshine and holidays.

Still, there are brighter things to look forward to – the Festival of Light at Diwali and the joy of Christmas.

After that there will be the coming of a new year, with spring not far behind.

Activity

I'm going to make some special places, which some of you can visit on our behalf.

Make three places around the hall with the white sheets of paper on the floor. At the front of the hall, place the (unlit) candle.

Now, I need three volunteers to be in a procession.

Line up the three volunteers at the front.

First, I have something here that we used in the warm days of summer.

A pair of sunglasses to remind us of those lovely sunny days when we needed to find the shade.

Who wore sunglasses during this summer?

Give the sunglasses to the first volunteer.

Here is something we will use during the winter – a scarf for when the weather gets cold and we need to wrap up against the biting wind.

Give the scarf to the second volunteer.

Here, to remind us of autumn, some fallen leaves.

At this time of the year, the trees keep their strength during the winter by losing their leaves.

Autumn is the time of fallen leaves. In some countries, it is called 'the Fall'.

Give the leaves to the third volunteer.

Now let's think about the change – the turning of the year – as our procession moves and places these reminders in three places around the hall.

They will walk very slowly and in silence.

First, to the place of the autumn leaves.

As they come to the place of the autumn leaves, *(name of volunteer)* will place the leaves gently down on the white paper. There.

For a moment, we will look at that place and think quietly about the trees. Think how green and beautiful they are when they blossom in the spring and summer and how stark and bare they are in the winter.

The procession moves slowly on now. It comes to the place of the symbols of summer. *(Name of volunteer)* puts down the sunglasses to remind us of the good times we had in the summer. There.

For a moment, we look at that place and think of the good times we had, in school and with our families and friends during the long, warm days of summer.

Now the procession moves on again to the place of the symbols of winter.

(Name of volunteer) puts down the scarf that reminds us of the coming winter – of cold winds, the feeling of being wrapped up in warm clothes and being snug in warm homes.

Let's just think of that for a while.

Now as our procession comes to the front of the hall again, let's also think of other parts of our world.

 ISBN 1 874050 55 4

Changing seasons

Let's think of people in Australia and New Zealand. Some of you have relatives or friends there.

In their assemblies, they will be giving thanks for the coming of spring.

The snow will be melting on the high peaks of the New Zealand mountains and the grassy plains will be showing green under spring rains.

Let's think, too, of India and of the coming of the monsoon rains. They are due about now.

Our assembly would be different again if we had it there. We would be looking for rain to bring new growth and to relieve us from six months of dry and dusty heat.

Here, at the front of the hall, is the most special place of all, where our candle stands waiting to be lit.

The procession will stand facing you and I will light the candle.

Light the candle.

This flame – a small light in a large room – reminds us that even though the nights are growing dark and the weather growing cold, there is brightness still to come.

Soon it will be Diwali – the Festival of Light. Then Christmas with its light and hope.

Always, in the darkness, there is a small light to guide us.

Let's imagine the light of this candle spreading out from here and shining across the Earth to the beautiful autumn scenery of New England in America, to the spring which is just beginning in New Zealand and to the coming rain in northern India.

We truly are one planet.

Have a moment of silence.

A prayer

Dear God, we thank you for the changing seasons as they move across the face of the Earth. We remember the good times of summer and we look forward to the light that will be brought into our lives by the great festivals of Diwali and Christmas. Help us to remember the messages of those festivals – of the power of good to drive out evil and of the power of light to conquer the darkness in the world. Amen.

A thought

Simple things remind us of good times we have had together and of other good times still to come. Let us remember that as darkness comes to us, light comes to our brothers and sisters all across our planet.

Song suggestions

'Look for signs that summer's done', *Someone's Singing Lord*

'Autumn', *Primary Assembly Song Book*, 13

Optional follow up

- Expand this assembly into a study of the seasons and the effect of the movement of the planet.
- Ask children to write a poem about the moods different seasons engender.

Dinosaurs

Assembly 3 of 4

This assembly points out in a poetic way that the living world has not always been as it is now. Dinosaurs once lived, and now do not. The wonders of nature have a time dimension – they come and go – as well as a spatial one.

You will need

- the OHT provided.

Taken by ....

Date ....

Given to ....

Comments

- ....
- ....
- ....

✦ Introduction

Today we will look at some real animals that don't exist now, but once did. These huge creatures lived once on our Earth – can you guess what they might be?

Long ago, when the Earth was much younger than it is now, and long before there were people on the Earth, there were dinosaurs.

Can we imagine what it must have been like then? No human beings, and so no towns, houses, roads, or any signs at all of humans living there. Not even a human footprint.

Yet the Earth was not empty. Far from it.

There were many plants and trees, and there were many animals. The king of the animals was the dinosaur.

There were, of course, many kinds of dinosaur.

There were small ones, perhaps the size of dogs and cats.

There were huge ones, with great long necks and massive bodies and long tails.

There were many medium-sized ones – the size of horses, perhaps.

Remember, there were no human eyes to see these strange and wonderful beasts. Nobody to peep at them round a rock, or to hide in a tree and look down. Nobody to stand in the shadow of a huge animal, or to dodge out of the way of its thundering feet.

Can we imagine what it might have been like to see the dinosaurs?

Can we imagine a long and slow-moving Diplodocus, with a mighty body and a tiny head on a long neck?

Here is a picture of him.

Put up the OHT provided.

What did he think about as he lumbered along? Was he just searching for food to keep his huge body going?

Can we imagine the mighty Tyrannosaurus Rex, fierce and terrifying, towering up on hind

Dinosaurs

legs, racing across the ground in search of smaller creatures to eat?

They were really there you know. The dinosaurs are not made up for stories in books. There really were these astonishing animals, walking the Earth and living their lives, more years ago than we can possibly imagine.

Had you been there you would have seen how real they were – you could have touched one or been brushed aside by it as it went past.

Diplodocus might have swung his head down from the sky to have a good look at you.

Tyrannosaurus Rex might have chased you until you hid up a tree.

But long before there were human beings, the dinosaurs disappeared. One by one they died, and no new ones were born.

They came and went before we had the chance to see them.

We all like to think about dinosaurs. We might even dream about them. This poem is about that.

📖 Poem

Where did you come from dinosaur?
And when it was over, where did you go?
I wish I could see the things that you saw
In that distant time, so long ago.

What did you feel like dinosaur
When you left your prints in the sand?
Did you find the life you were looking for
In that far off younger land?

I wish I could meet you dinosaur
To check on the tales we are told.
Were you really as big as they say you were?
Were you fierce and fast and bold?

But I'll never see you dinosaur
Long ages keep us apart.
You're just a few pictures that once we saw
And a dream that lives on in my heart.

✦ Conclusion

Our Earth is a beautiful place, filled with plants, animals, birds, insects and fish. Which wonderful animals would you like to see? A lion? A tiger? A kangaroo?

Take suggestions.

What beautiful trees and tropical plants?

Take suggestions.

Would you like to see snow-capped mountains, glaciers and icebergs or tropical forests, deep valleys and mighty oceans?

Perhaps you have seen some of these things. Perhaps you will travel to the North Pole, or to the summit of Everest. The world is there for you. All of those things exist. They are not made up stories.

But there are some wonderful things that we will never see, because they are no longer on the Earth.

The extinct dinosaurs remind us that the world keeps changing. The wonders of creation are not just the things we can see now.

A prayer

Dear God, we thank you for the dinosaurs that once walked on the Earth. We pray that we human beings will always try to care for the animals and plants that share the Earth with us today. Amen.

A thought

If no human being has ever seen a dinosaur, how do we know what they looked like? We know from people who have studied remains and fossils. These people know how precious the Earth is, and how we can learn even from animals who died out long before human beings were on the planet.

Song suggestions

'A perfect world', Primary Assembly Song Book, 61

'When a dinosaur's feeling hungry', Tinder Box, 12

Dinosaurs

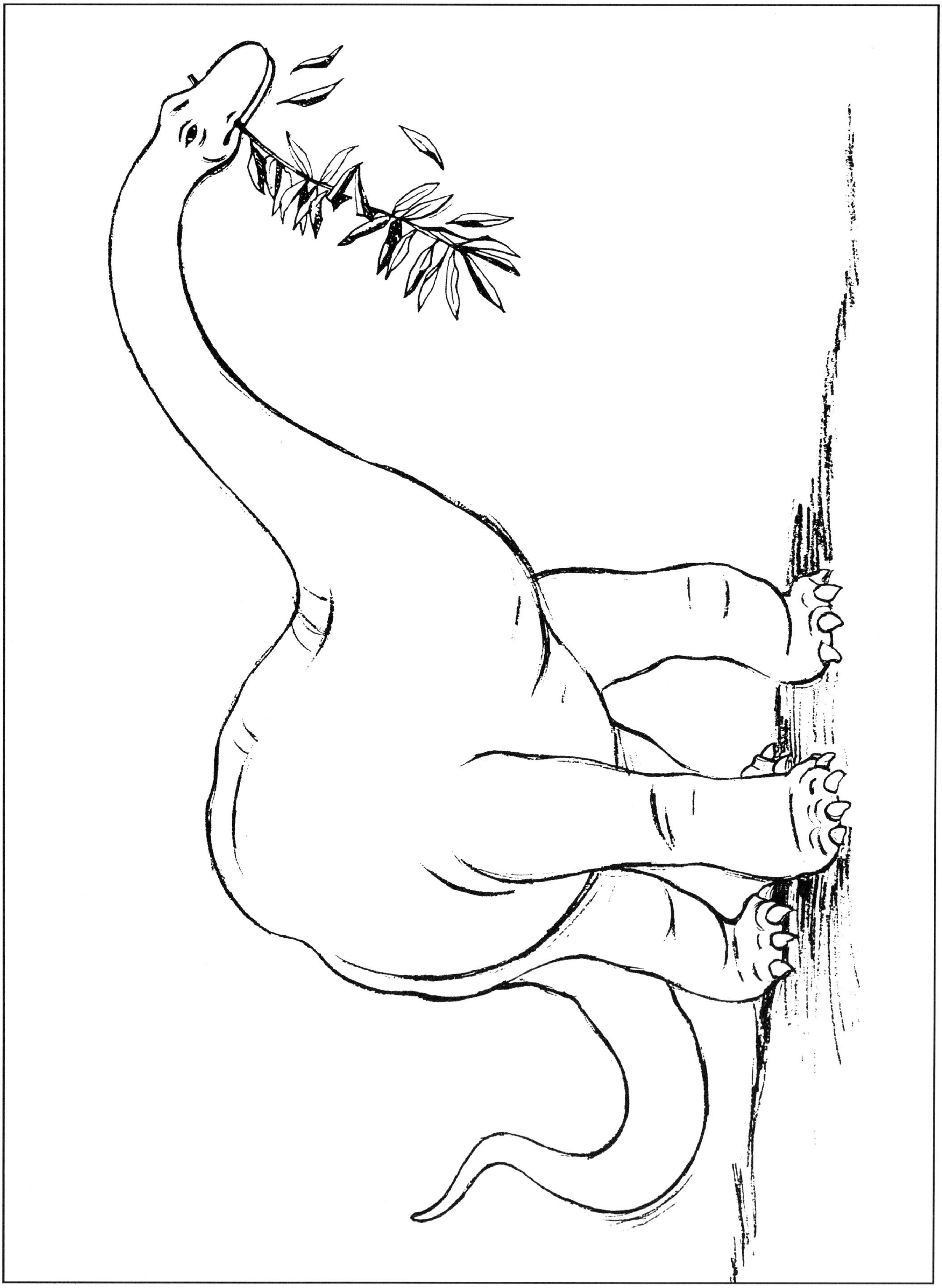

Planting trees

Assembly 4 of 4

This assembly is about young people and older people planting trees together. The presence of trees, which will outlive all the people there, speaks of continuity. It introduces children to thoughts about mortality and lasting value.

You will need

- the OHT provided.

Taken by ....

Date ....

Given to ....

Comments

- ....
- ....
- ....

✦ Introduction

Today we're going to think about the changes that happen to us in our lifetimes, and realise that some things will be here long after we are all gone.

Our neighbours had a sad time last week. Their old dog Jock finally died. He was fourteen, which is very old for a dog. It's not a long time for a human being, though. My neighbours remember him very well as a puppy, bouncing around. He was a lot of fun then, though they had to train him. Then when he was an adult dog, he was a good friend to the family, always pleased to see people, and ready to go out for a walk. We'd hear him barking sometimes, and we knew that he was getting ready to be taken out.

Then, when he got older, he slowed down, and he liked to lie behind the settee in the front room, or lie out in the sun in the garden. He'd get up sometimes and wander over to someone to have his neck scratched or his head stroked. He always liked that. Puppy, adult, old dog – he moved gently from one stage in his life to another, and at each stage he brought something special to the people around him. My neighbours might get a new dog eventually, but they'll never forget Jock.

Life comes and goes. Some creatures only live a short time. Others – elephants and tortoises for example – live a long time. Some trees, though, live a very long time indeed. There are trees standing not far from here that were here long before me, or my parents, and will still be here long after I or my own children have gone.

In our story today we meet Roberta and Gran as, together with some other people, they think about life on the Earth, its beginnings and its endings, and about the things that go on after we are gone.

🕮 Story

Roberta thought it was cool that she was going to Gran's residential home with her school. She had only ever been with her mum and her Auntie Sylvia before. She started going when she was quite small and Gran first went to the home. Gran was one of the oldest residents

Planting trees

now, and Roberta still liked to go on Saturdays.

Now, though, her school was taking part in a tree-planting project at the home, and she and about twelve of the other children were going down there to join in the ceremony.

Roberta was excited and kept telling the other children about the home – in fact, she was in danger of boring them to death about it! Sandeep would be particularly annoyed, because his gran was in the same place, and he knew just as much about it as Roberta did. 'Come on, Robbie!' he'd say. 'Tell us something we don't know.'

But they were all good friends, and they all looked forward to the tree-planting day.

When the day came, the twelve who were representing the school walked down to the residential home with their headteacher, Mrs James, and Mr Gordon, one of the classroom assistants. When they got there, the residents were already out in the sunshine, sitting on chairs facing the area where the trees were going to be planted. The trees were already placed in their holes, just waiting to have a bit of extra soil added and pressed down.

Roberta looked for her gran, and soon saw her and gave her a wave. Mr Gordon saw her waving and had a word with Mrs James, who said, 'Anyone who has a relative here can go and sit with them, if they want.' Sandeep and Roberta went over to their grans, and Delice, one of the staff at the home, found some chairs for them. Roberta settled down next to her gran, and the ceremony started.

Mrs James went to the front, because she'd been asked to give a short talk. 'Good morning everybody,' she started. 'This is a privilege for me. I'm looking now at groups of people of different generations – three, really – the children, the staff, and the residents. Together, we span an awfully long time. I know that at least one of you here was born at the beginning of the twentieth century. Many of these children here will still be here when planning begins for the one that starts in 2100 – perhaps they will even be around to see it, who knows. So between us we represent two hundred years of our world's history...'

When Mrs James's speech was finished, Roberta went forward with the other children, and, with some of the residents from the home, they helped some of the people from the parks department put soil round the base of the new trees.

Afterwards, the children and the residents had tea together in the garden. Roberta sat with her gran at a table with Sandeep and his gran.

'It was a good speech that your headmistress made,' said Roberta's gran. Mrs Rooprai, Sandeep's gran, agreed. Then she put down her teacup. 'When I was a girl in India,' she said, and Sandeep groaned. 'Oh, Gran,' he said. 'Not another India story.'

'Now you stop it,' said Roberta's gran. 'I like Veena's stories. You go on, dear,' she said.

'As I was saying,' said Mrs Rooprai. 'When I was a girl in India, my mother was cook to an English couple. They were very kind to me. One day, I was playing in the garden with their daughter Marjorie, when the lady came out to watch us. Soon we were tired with the heat, and we sat in the shade of a tree in the garden. The lady sat down on a chair which was there in the shade, and she called to my mother, who brought cool lemonade for us. The English lady drank her lemonade, and I always remember what she said – I think I have most of the words right.

'"Things will change here," she said. "You, Veena, will see a different India, with new ideas. Your life will be different from your mother's. Marjorie and I will go home to England and Marjorie's life will be different from mine. None of us can even dream of what the future will bring for you, Veena, still less for your own children."

'Then she looked up at the tree and said, "But this tree will still be here when you are grown up, and we are far away. Perhaps, when you yourself are old you will come here and remember the times we had together."'

'And did you?' asked Roberta.

Mrs Rooprai smiled. 'Well as you see, dear, I am here now, and not where the tree is. But I did visit it many times after Marjorie and her mother had gone. And when I came to England forty years ago, I carried the memory of the tree in my mind, and I still visit it in my heart.'

'There are new trees now, Gran!' said Sandeep.

'New trees, new life, new memories,' said Roberta's gran. 'These trees, too, will be here long after we are gone. You two might visit them and remember today, and the other days we have had together in this place. Or, of course, you may be far away and able to visit them only in your mind.'

Put up the OHT provided.

'But we are specially lucky,' said Mrs Rooprai, 'because, although the tree is just a memory now, the friendship we had then has become very real again in old age. I think it is a sort of miracle, do you not think so Marjorie?' And Roberta's gran smiled and put her hand on Mrs Rooprai's. 'I think so, Veena,' she said.

✦ Conclusion

A tree is a very strong symbol of life. It starts as a small seed, and it grows slowly and surely over many years, becoming more beautiful all the time. It reflects the changing seasons, from the green of spring, through the gold of autumn to the cold, bare branches of winter. Each tree will see many seasons like that – perhaps hundreds of them. Around it, the world will change. People will be born, seek the shade of the tree, grow old and leave the Earth, and new people will come to do the same. Life goes on.

A prayer

Lord, we thank you for giving us the life that lies before us. May we always make the most of what we have, always making new starts, always searching for the next thing we have to do. Help us to keep our memories safe and precious in our hearts, and to value the friendships we make along the way. Amen.

A thought

You plant a seed in the ground, and one day your children and your grandchildren will see a beautiful tree.

Song suggestions

'God who made the Earth', *Come and Praise*, 10

'I've got a memory of you', *Primary Assembly Song Book*, 47

Optional follow up

Visit some young trees in the school grounds or a park. Try to imagine them fully grown, and try to describe what might be going on around them.

Planting trees

Working together

Assembly 1 of 4

This assembly is based on making a cup of tea. It is a reminder of the way that our lives depend on work of people across the world.

You will need

- a kettle and extension lead
- a teapot
- a cup and saucer
- some milk, a teabag and some sugar
- a bowl to catch the water
- a timer

Try to boil the kettle before the assembly so that it boils faster when you need it.

Taken by ....

Date ....

Given to ....

Comments

- ....
- ....
- ....

✦ Activity

Before I start today, I feel like a cup of tea.

You don't mind if I just make one, do you? I'm making it for a special reason.

Make the tea, keeping up a running commentary, also humming to yourself and so on. The children will pay attention for a surprisingly long time to all of this.

Right. What's my checklist?

First, kettle on.

When it's hot, warm the pot with a little hot water and then empty waste water into the bowl.

Tea bag in the pot.

Water on the tea.

Leave it to brew for two minutes.

Use a timer to keep the children's interest.

I'm using a tea bag because it's quick and easy. Some people like proper tea, made with tea leaves.

Who has tea made with tea leaves in their house?

Take responses if appropriate. Some children will have, especially if they are from particular ethnic communities.

Milk in the cup.

Pour the tea.

Add sugar.

Ah! All ready to have my cup of tea now!

Working together

Sit down and drink the tea in a relaxed way.

Who could have done that? I can't ask you to do it, because I can't ask you to handle the boiling water in the hall here.

So I made a cup of tea. I *made* a cup of tea. Or did I?

Did I make the water?

Did I make the cup?

Did I make the milk?

Did I make the sugar?

Did I make the tea bag?

No, of course not.

The tea came from India.

The water came from the water mains and I got it from the tap.

The milk came from a cow and was brought here by the milkman.

The sugar was made from sugar beet, which grows in the ground. It was taken from the sugar beet and put into bags in a factory.

So much went on to make that cup of tea possible.

So many people worked hard – tea pickers in India, sugar beet workers in Cambridgeshire, water company workers who make sure that leaks are mended and that the water keeps flowing, pottery workers who made the cup and the saucer.

Other people did the work.

Did all those people work together in one place? Did they all know each other?

No, they worked in different parts of the world, thousands of miles apart. But every one of them was important.

If one had not done their job, I would not have had my cup of tea.

If the tea picker had not picked the tea. If the farmer had not milked the cow. If the sugar beet farmer had not picked sugar beet. If the water company engineers had not kept up the supply of water. I would not have had a cup of tea.

Sometimes, when I drink a cup of tea, I forget those hard-working people across the world.

I should look into the cup and see a tea picker, working the in heat and humidity of India, a farmer, up at five o'clock in the morning in his milking parlour, a sugar beet farmer driving his crop along the road behind a tractor in the pouring rain, a water company engineer out on a cold Sunday night to mend a burst water main.

All so that I can enjoy my cup of tea.

So I should thank them, shouldn't I?

✦ Conclusion

We should be grateful for all the people whose hard work makes such a difference to the way we live our lives.

Remember I said that I was making a cup of tea for a special reason?

It was because a cup of tea is one of the simplest ways to remind ourselves that, all over our planet, we all depend on each other.

Sometimes without even knowing about it, people help each other.

The Earth is our home, we have nowhere else to go. We all live on just one planet. It is our duty to look after it and to look after each other.

A prayer

Dear God, we remember today the many millions of people on our planet who are at work, earning a living for their families and helping each other to have all the things we take for granted. We remember farmers, pickers, drivers, office workers and so many others. We remember especially those people in our own families who are at work today. Keep them safe and happy in their work. Amen.

A thought

All over our planet, so many jobs depend on each other. The tea pickers' tea leaves would pile up uselessly if there was no transport and no tea factory. The checkout worker at the supermarket would have nothing to do if the lorry drivers did not keep bringing new supplies to the back of the supermarket. We all depend on each other.

Song suggestions

'Everything', *Primary Assembly Song Book*, 4

'Sing a song of people', *Tinder Box*, 18

The day the heating broke down

It's chilly outside.
Jack Frost's been about.
And we do not enjoy
the cold weather.
But in here we're warm.
And until we go out,
We'll be comfy and
cosy together.

The day the heating broke down

Assembly 2 of 4

This assembly shows how people work together to put things right when they go wrong and demonstrates how adults will often work a little harder to help when children are in difficulty.

You will need

- a day when it's quite cold outside, but warm indoors
- the OHT provided.

Taken by ....

Date ....

Given to ....

Comments

- ....
- ....
- ....

✦ Introduction

Is anybody cold? No, we're nice and warm in here.

Can we pretend we're cold? What would we do if we were cold? We'd be saying, 'Brrr' and hugging ourselves.

But it's not cold, it's cosy in here. Why is that? Because the heating is on. Why is the heating on? Because *(name)* the caretaker looks after the boilers and makes sure that the heating comes on to warm the school up before we come in each morning.

The caretaker is someone who helps keep our school running smoothly. Today we are going to think about the work the caretaker does and about the other people who help in maintaining our school.

Here are some words about being warm inside when it's cold outside.

Put up the OHT provided.

I'll say them first and then we'll say them together.

Read out the poem and then ask the children to read it with you.

Why are we warm in here? Because we have the heating on. We just take the heating for granted don't we? Yet there are people who make sure it works.

What would happen if the heating went off on a cold day? It would gradually get colder and colder. It might get so cold that we couldn't carry on with our work.

It looked like that might happen at Sidney Street School, in our story today. Luckily, though, there were good people who worked hard to put things right.

🕮 Story

It was a Monday morning at Sidney Street School. All the classes were busy.

There were groups of children on the carpet in the corridor reading. There were some Reception children in aprons doing something wet at the sink.

The day the heating broke down

Little Amanda was missing her aunty and was sitting on the secretary's knee.

Erasmus, the school cat was on the window ledge outside the kitchen, hoping to get in, although he never succeeded.

Mrs Wilson, the headteacher, was hearing some readers in her room.

Mrs Richards, the cook, was starting the fish fingers.

Mr Jenkins the caretaker was round the back of the school picking up a bit of litter.

Everything was quite normal.

Then, suddenly, something happened. Lots of people noticed it, but at first nobody really knew what it was. There was something unusual – a new sound, perhaps. What was it?

Mrs Wilson looked up. Mrs Richards stopped unwrapping the cartons of fish fingers. Erasmus lifted his head and looked around.

The secretary looked away from little Amanda for a moment to see what had happened.

It was Mrs Wilson who realised first. What she had heard, she realised was not a new sound, but a new silence.

Usually, all around the school, in the classrooms, in the corridors, in the offices, was a gentle background humming sound that came from the pipes and radiators. It was the sound of the heating pumps, pushing hot water around the school to keep everybody warm.

That sound had stopped.

Mrs Wilson sat for a moment with her head on one side, listening. Then she said, 'Oh my goodness, the heating's gone off!'

Quickly she sent her readers back to class, then she went out into the corridor, calling for the caretaker.

Mr Jenkins was always the first person she called when there was trouble with the building and its fittings.

'Mr Jenkins!' she called. 'Where are you? What's going on?'

Mr Jenkins was just coming in the back door. He heard Mrs Wilson calling and hurried through to see what she wanted.

'The heating's gone off!' she said. 'It's freezing cold outside! I can feel it getting colder in here already. What can you do?'

Mr Jenkins hurried off to the boiler room. He was back in no time.

'I don't know what the problem is,' he said as he shook his head. 'We'll have to ring Mr Webster, the heating engineer.'

All the time it was getting colder.

The Reception children started to feel it. Next door, 2W stopped getting changed for PE.

Mr Jenkins spoke to Mr Webster, who promised to come out to the school straightaway.

'Hurry!' said Mr Jenkins. 'It's getting cold already.'

Mrs Wilson thought she might have to send all the children home. This was a really difficult job, because she would have to contact all the parents and have the children picked up. They were too young just to be sent out of school. She dreaded the thought of having to do it.

She went for a walk round the school, making sure all the doors and windows were shut to keep the heat in. She told the children they could wear their coats.

The day the heating broke down

Still it was getting colder. The Reception children put their coats on, but they still said, 'Brrr', and hugged themselves with their arms. In 2W, the children were jumping up and down with their teacher, trying to keep warm.

At last Mr Webster's car drew up and Mr Webster went straight to the boiler room with a bag of tools and instruments.

He did some tapping and fiddling, while Mr Jenkins looked on anxiously.

In school, all the time it was getting colder.

The Reception children started to hug each other and in 2W the children jumped up and down even higher.

Mr Webster said it needed someone from the boiler factory to come. Mr Jenkins reported to Mrs Wilson. Mrs Wilson rang the boiler factory.

'We can come tomorrow,' they said.

'Oh!' said Mrs Wilson. 'But that's a real problem. I have two hundred young children here and I may have to get them all picked up and taken home.'

The man at the boiler factory had a think about that. He had a little girl at school and he knew what it must be like for Mrs Wilson.

After a few moments, he said, 'OK then. I'll come now. Expect me in half an hour.'

Sure enough, in only half an hour, the man from the boiler factory had arrived and was in the boiler room.

He tapped and fiddled, while Mr Jenkins and Mr Webster looked on anxiously.

Suddenly he stepped back and wiped his hands on a cloth.

'Try that!' he said.

Mr Jenkins stepped up to the big red button that switched the heating on. He looked at Mr Webster and he looked at the man from the boiler factory. Then he took a deep breath and pressed the big red button.

For a moment, there was silence.

Then, deep inside the machinery came a dull 'whooomp', as the boiler lit up.

Mr Jenkins looked through a little glass window and saw the bright blue flame.

'Try the pumps,' said Mr Webster.

Mr Jenkins pressed two more buttons. The pumps started up immediately and the three men laughed with relief.

Inside the school, Mrs Wilson stopped what she was doing as she listened to the familiar sound again – the pumps had started up.

She cheered and stopped planning to send all the children home.

Meanwhile, in the school, it was gradually getting warmer.

The Reception children stopped hugging each other. In 2W, the children stopped jumping round the classroom and stood around puffing and panting.

Mr Webster, Mr Jenkins and the man from the boiler factory came to see Mrs Wilson.

They all had a cup of tea together.

The day the heating broke down

'A job well done!' said Mrs Wilson and the three men beamed with satisfaction.

'Can't let the children down,' said the man from the boiler factory. 'That's right,' said Mr Webster. 'Where there are children involved, we all make a special effort.'

'Well thank you very much,' said Mrs Wilson as she passed round the biscuits.

✦ Conclusion

We take it for granted that our school will be warm and comfortable – that the taps, electricity switches and the window openers will work.

If something does go wrong, we hope that someone will put it right for us. Usually, people try very hard to help when there are children involved.

Did you know that everyone, all around, sees you as in a way belonging to them? You are everybody's children, very special and very precious. When there is trouble, everyone will try to help.

Jesus taught us about helping other people. He told the story of the Good Samaritan, which is about helping someone even if you don't particularly like them.

He was also very sure that all adults have a duty to help children. Once when he was preaching, some of the adults tried to shoo children away, but he stopped them.

He asked the children to come forward to be near to him.

'Let the little children come to me,' he said as he put his hands on them and blessed them.

He did not like to see children chased away and not listened to, and neither do we in school.

A prayer

Dear God, we thank you for all who work to keep our school open, warm and working well. We thank you for people who are taking care of us and who want to help us. We rejoice that there are so many of these people. Be with all our friends in their work today and always. Amen.

A thought

Children are the future. Adults realise that and make a special effort to look after children and keep them safe and happy.

Song suggestions

'A perfect world', *Primary Assembly Song Book*, 61

'When I needed a neighbour', *Someone's Singing Lord,* 35

Optional follow up idea

Talk about the charities set up for children and their special role in society. if possible, ask a worker from a children's charity or for another adult involved in caring specifically for children (for example, a children's nurse) to talk about why they have chosen to do so.

The ceremony of food

Assembly 3 of 4

This assembly demonstrates the benefits of working together. It shows that by sharing what we have, we can make something richer and more worthwhile than we can individually.

You will need

- some stones in a pan of water
- a loaf of bread (preferably a crusty loaf, but any bread will do)

Taken by ....

Date ....

Given to ....

Comments

- ....
- ....
- ....

✦ Introduction

Today's assembly is a very old traditional tale about a group of people who found that by sharing what they had they all enjoyed a good meal.

Show the pan of water and stones.

This is a pan of water.

What are these? Yes, they are stones.

As you tell this story, use the pan and the stones, together with some mime, to illustrate it.

I am going to tell you the story of the man who made stone soup. Yes, you heard it right – soup from stones. Sounds ridiculous? Well listen carefully.

🕮 Story

Once there was a man who was on a long journey, lasting many days. On his back was a pack with just a few clothes and a little food. Hanging from his pack was the big saucepan in which he cooked his food.

One day this man, weary from travelling, came to a large village. As he entered the village he saw that the people were all busy about their daily tasks – tending animals and crops, cleaning their houses, mending their walls and gates and fences. He greeted some of the people, who spoke to him politely enough, but without much warmth in their voices.

He shrugged his shoulders. He had been in such villages many times. He thought that he would eat his food and move on.

So he sat down by the well in the village. He took off his pack, unclipped his saucepan, and drew himself some water from the well. He poured the water in the pan.

Then he walked to the edge of the village, to the beginning of the woods and gathered some firewood. He returned and lit his fire, using his flint and steel.

He put his saucepan to boil on the fire, then he searched in his pack for some food to cook – a few onions, perhaps, or some cabbage. But to his horror he found nothing. He had eaten all of his food. There was nothing left.

The ceremony of food

He looked around. The people in the village had probably noticed his problem, but they all looked the other way and got on with their jobs. It seemed that they did not want to help.

Then the man had an idea.

He walked around the edge of the village and picked up a few stones from the ground. He polished them clean with a piece of cloth from his pack. He put them into the pan and settled down to watch them boil.

Two of the men of the village had watched him do this and they came towards him.

'What are you doing?' they asked him.

'Why!' said the traveller. 'I am making a fine soup.'

'But you are boiling only stones!' exclaimed the men of the village.

'That is true,' said the traveller. 'But I will make a fine soup nevertheless.'

He went quiet again and watched his stone soup boiling on the fire.

One of the village men cleared his throat. He was very curious.

'Can I taste the fine stone soup when it is done?' he asked.

The traveller looked up and frowned.

'But you have contributed nothing to the soup,' he said to the man. 'I am a hungry traveller. Why should I give you my fine soup?'

The village man thought for a moment.

Then he said, 'If I add something to the soup, may I taste it?'

The traveller nodded. 'It is of no matter to me. If you add to the soup, then you can eat your share.'

So the village man went away and came back with a very large onion, which he dropped into the soup. The other village man who was with him watched. Then he went away and came back with some pieces of turnip.

'If I add these, may I try the fine stone soup?' he asked.

The traveller nodded.

Soon other village people gathered round.

'What is this traveller doing?' they asked.

The first village man replied, 'He is making soup from stones.'

The other villagers laughed.

'You cannot make soup from stones,' said one of the women. 'Come, let us taste it and we will see that it is no use at all.'

The first village man said, 'Ah, but in order to taste the soup you must first add something to it. That is only fair, because this man is a hungry traveller.'

The woman hurried off to find something to add to the soup. She came back with a piece of meat from her larder, which she added to the soup.

Soon other villagers were adding things in the hope of being able to eat the fine stone soup. One put in a carrot. Another some potatoes. Another some chicken bones.

After a while the traveller's pan was filled with a fine mixture of meat and vegetables – and a few stones.

The stone soup boiled for a long time and the villagers could not wait to taste it.

When it was finished, they lined up with their cups and the traveller gave each of them a small portion of the soup.

'This is a fine stone soup, indeed,' they all agreed.

The traveller smiled.

'Think what you have done,' he said to them. 'You have all added richness to my soup. You have all tasted the richness from it. My soup was thin, poor stuff, but together, each in a small way, you have added goodness to it. Now you share that goodness.'

The villagers nodded.

The traveller continued, 'Think how you could easily have helped any weary traveller without being asked. Think how you could always help each other by sharing what you have. Give thanks to God for the way you have discovered the joy of sharing, and saved me from going hungry.'

✦ Conclusion

That story uses food as a symbol for sharing. Many stories do that. The story was about soup, which is an important food for many people.

Now look at this loaf of bread. This is also an important food. Throughout history, across large parts of the world, bread has been more than just something to make sandwiches with.

Bread is a sign of God's goodness, with his gifts to us of nature and the Earth.

The seed is sown in the ground – wheat, rye, barley. It is warmed by the sun and watered by the rain, so that it grows. Then it can be harvested and the grains are ground into flour. The flour is mixed with water and brought to life by yeast.

The mixture is baked in an oven to make the beautiful crusty product that we call bread – made by the hands of men and women, but made possible by the goodness of God and by the gifts of nature.

When a family or a group of friends sits down together and shares bread together, then something else is added. That is the love of family and friends for each other.

In this way the simple loaf of bread becomes a powerful sign of love and friendship.

That is why sharing bread has religious importance for many people. Christians share bread in their communion services, and think of bread as representing the presence of Jesus among them.

I'm going to choose a group of you to show this, and to help us to celebrate the love of God, the gifts of nature and the richness of our friendship for each other.

Choose a symbolic group of six or eight volunteers. Sit them down in a circle and put the loaf of bread in the middle of them.

This bread is a sign of God's goodness towards us. God, we thank you for all of your gifts – for food, the riches of the Earth, but most of all for friendship, love and regard

The ceremony of food

which we have for each other. Think of this bread as representing the love of Jesus, who shared bread with His disciples.

Now who will break the bread and give a small piece to each of the others?

Choose one volunteer and help him or her to break the bread and give it to the others. Take and eat some yourself.

Today, as the day goes on, when there are difficulties between us, let's all try to remember this moment which we all had together, of when we were bound together.

A prayer

Dear God, we do so many things together. We work together, we play together and we eat together. Help us to concentrate on the things that bring us together, and not to dwell on the things that drive us apart. For the things that unite us are always stronger than the things that divide us. Amen.

A thought

Sharing food – even handing round a bag of sweets – acts as cement. It keeps us close together.

Song suggestions

'The family of man', *Come and Praise*, 69

Optional follow up

Act out the story of the stone soup.

Joining together

Assembly 4 of 4

This assembly is about some children practising a three-legged race with their parents. The aim is to run efficiently, and to investigate whether three legs are better than two. The message is that working together requires patience and a lot of understanding.

You will need

- a long handkerchief or similar to tie two children's legs together, three-legged race style
- two volunteers.

Taken by ....

Date ....

Given to ....

Comments

- ....
- ....
- ....

✦ Introduction

Today's assembly will show us the importance of working well together – in a three-legged race, the two partners must make their legs which are tied together, move at the same time – otherwise they will fall over. Our assembly tells about some children and their parents who tried to work together in a three-legged race.

Do you know what a three-legged race is? It's when two people stand side by side, and you tie one leg of one person to one leg of the other. Then they have to try to run and race other pairs of people.

Let me show you.

Demonstrate with two volunteers. Show how they need to be firmly linked by arms round waists or shoulders. Take care they don't fall over, but just show how difficult it is, and how they need to establish a rhythm by watching and understanding how each is moving.

Can you see why this is difficult? It's quite easy for one person to run along. And it's easy for someone to run alongside them. But if you tie their legs together, suddenly it's not so easy. Why is that? It's because each person runs in a slightly different way – one may have a longer stride, or take shorter steps. They have to keep absolutely together.

If they are very different in size it's even more difficult. Suppose we tie a small child to a big adult?

Try this. Show how difficult it is.

🕮 Story

'Dad,' said Mark, one Monday evening after tea. 'At the school sports this year we are having a three-legged race for children and parents. You team up with one of your parents and each ties one leg to one of the other person's legs. Then they have a race.'

'Does it matter which two legs you tie together?' asked his sister Simone, sounding very interested. 'Of course it does, lunatic!' said Mark. 'It has to be the two nearest to each other. If you tied the other two it would be...'

Joining together

'A lot more interesting,' said Simone.

'Well, anyway,' said Mark. 'Darren and me think that with three legs going you are bound to be faster – three legs must be faster than two.'

His dad sucked his teeth and shook his head. 'Can't see that, old son,' he said. 'I think you'd be falling over all the time.'

'Well, Dad,' said Mark. 'We'll be able to find out, won't we, because...'

'Hang on!' said Dad. 'You're not expecting me to do this are you?'

Simone joined in. 'Oh yes, and Mum and me are going to challenge you. As a matter of fact, we've already put all four of our names down.'

Dad groaned. Mum grinned and rubbed her hands together, and winked at Simone.

The next evening, when they were all at home, they went into the garden, with big handkerchiefs to tie round their legs. 'Mustn't use string or anything like that,' said Mum, 'because it could hurt us.'

They stood in a row, four people in two pairs. Eight legs – well, six if you counted the tied together legs as one.

Simone started them off. 'Ready, set, GO!' she shouted. All four of them lunged forward, and after two staggering steps all four of them collapsed full length onto the grass. There were shrieks of laughter, and then even more laughter again when they tried to stand up.

In the end they had to untie their legs before they could stand up.

'How did I get into this?' said Dad. 'I could be inside watching the football.'

'Oh Dad, come on,' said Simone. 'Be a sport. All we need to do is practise.'

So practise is what they did, for the rest of that evening, and for the next two evenings. There was a lot of laughter, a lot of falling down and a lot of grumbling. They realised that the secret was first to hold on tightly to each other so that instead of two bodies they were like one body, and also to take steps that were not too long for the smallest person in the pair. They also learned to set up a rhythm, so that nobody was taken by surprise by a change of pace.

By the end of the week, Dad was no longer grumpy. He had the light of battle in his eyes. 'Right!' he said, as they went indoors after the final training session. 'I can't wait for the race. My son and I will annihilate the opposition. Whatever that means.'

'Don't be so sure,' said Mum. 'The women of this family are a force to be reckoned with.'

Sports Day was on the Friday afternoon of that week. Simone and Mark were impatient all morning, but the afternoon eventually came and everyone went out onto the field, and the parents started arriving. Simone and Mark's mum and dad waved to them from their place on the other side of the field.

There were lots of races – a sack race, some skipping races, and nobody worried too much who won, because every child got a little prize of some sort. Then, at last, came the three-legged race for parents and children.

It was the funniest race that anyone had ever seen, and it took about a quarter of an hour instead of the few seconds that it should have taken, because everything happened – people fell over, or their handkerchief came undone and had to be tied up again. And, of course, some people were really making a good joke of it – when Mark and his dad fell and untied their handkerchief, Mark's dad tied himself up to one of the other dads and they ran to the end of the course, and then had to come back and start all over again with the right partners.

The successful pairs, of course, were the ones who had really practised and got the hang of it. Simone and her mum were very good. So good that when they finished they kept on running. 'We'll do a lap of honour!' gasped Simone's mum and they ran all round the field with everyone cheering.

In the end, nobody knew who had won, or even if anyone had won at all. Everyone got a chocolate bar, which kept them happy. What they had discovered, though, was just how much patience and practise were needed when people were trying to work together to do something.

✦ Conclusion

Is there anything we do in school that's like a three-legged race? Suppose I asked you to work together in pairs on your reading. Would that be like it? Well, at least you wouldn't fall over. But you might find that you had to go at the speed of the other person. You might find that your partner could read for longer chunks of time than you, or liked to go in short bursts with gaps in between.

Or suppose you were working together on a maths problem, measuring water in containers and writing down what you find out. You might find that, while the other person is slow and careful, you want to be quick and get on with it.

When that happens you have to think of the three-legged race – imagine you're tied together with a handkerchief and you have to find a way of working together. Once you do settle down to the same speed, then you'll make good progress.

As human beings we want to do well. We want to beat the other person. That's often a good thing, but it's good, too, that we can work with someone else to do better.

A prayer

Lord, help us to work well with other people. Give us patience and understanding as we do our work and play together, and as we live together in our homes. Amen.

A thought

The old saying goes, 'Two heads are better than one'. It means that if two people think about a problem, then they can get the answer more quickly. But they need to be patient with each other all the same.

Song suggestions

'For all the strength we have', *Someone's Singing Lord*, 16

'Friends', *Primary Assembly Song Book*, 83

Optional follow up

Try having some three-legged races in the hall or on the field. Use them to discuss the benefits of cooperation, and the need for give and take.

 ISBN 1 874050 55 4

A spooky summer fair

Assembly 1 of 4

This describes being frightened for fun but also points out that many children live in very genuine fear. There is reference to the need to disclose genuine fear caused by people in school or in the family.

You will need

- nothing at all.

Taken by ....

Date ....

Given to ....

Comments

- ....
- ....

✦ Introduction

Right. I'm going to frighten everybody now.

Make a frightening face and say 'Boo!'

Did that frighten you? No?

What are you all laughing at? You're supposed to be very frightened.

Who thinks they can come out here and frighten everybody this morning?

Take some volunteers and have fun with this for a few minutes.

Now, perhaps we can all frighten each other. Turn to the person next to you and be really scary.

Well, nobody seemed to be frightened did they? It was all good fun really.

Sometimes being frightened can be good fun. Here's a story about that.

🕮 Story

One morning, in assembly, Mrs MacKenzie had a special announcement to make. 'We're having a summer fair again this year. There'll be the usual sorts of things – stalls, games, horse rides and a bouncy castle. But this year we're going to try something different. We want each class to come up with an idea for a stall. It can be anything at all within reason – we'll have to be sure it's safe and sensible of course. The idea is to make some money and have some fun as well. Over the next few weeks I want you to think about it with your teachers.'

Back in class, Mr Deacon asked everyone to think of ideas. 'I have a few myself,' he said. 'We could make things to sell, perhaps, or make a game. But it would be good if you could think of some things for yourselves. Talk to your parents at home and see if they will help you, and we will discuss it again tomorrow.'

The next day, when Mr Deacon had called the register, he sat everyone on the carpet to talk about summer fair ideas. 'Who's had some ideas?' he asked.

Everyone looked at each other and a few hands went up. Mr Deacon listened to the ideas. John thought they should make some sweets and he had a recipe. Paul wanted to bring in his football game and charge money for it. Bimal suggested using the class computer to play games on.

A spooky summer fair

Then Lewis put his hand up. 'Sir, my mum had an idea and I thought it was really good.'

'Go on then, Lewis, tell us all about it,' said Mr Deacon.

'When she was at school in St Lucia, she remembers that on Creole Day they had a Spooky Room.'

Everyone laughed at that. 'What on earth's that, Lewis?' asked Mr Deacon. He was laughing too.

'Well, they blacked out their classroom, so it was dark inside, and then they made it really frightening. Some of them dressed up in sheets, and they made big pictures of skeletons. Somebody had some flashing lights, and there was spooky music as well. Everyone paid to come in.'

Everyone laughed again at that and started talking to each other with big grins on their faces. Mr Deacon looked around and he knew from the way the class was excited that this was probably a good idea. It sounded like something that would keep them all busy, too, and not just involve a few chosen people.

'Right!' he said. 'Let's have a think about this. For one thing I'm not too sure our classroom is the right place. Even with the blinds down it won't be dark enough on a summer afternoon. We'll have to think of somewhere else in the school, if we're going to do it at all. And what if it's all too ghostly and frightening?'

Lewis had the answer to that. 'Sir, my mum said that nobody really thought it was serious. They knew it was the kids dressed up and they just had a big laugh.'

So, Mr Deacon had a word with Mrs MacKenzie next time she came down to the classroom. She thought it was funny, too, and she went away shaking her head and laughing.

The class set to work. They made all sorts of fun things – skeletons that danced on strings, face masks, long worms made out of folded paper and big insects cut out of card.

The day before the fair, the whole class went down to the empty classroom in the older part of the school. It would be easier to make it dark there. They arranged desks so that anyone coming in had to walk around in a sort of a zigzag. Then they had a practise. Some of the class jiggled models on strings, some dressed up with masks and popped up from behind desks. Some put sheets on and waved their arms. Even in broad daylight it was good fun. In the dark, with flashing lights and sound effects it would be even better.

On the day of the fair, Mr Deacon set up a desk outside the room and sat behind it charging 20p to go in. 'Frighten yourself silly in our Spooky Room!' he shouted.

The first person to go in was Mrs O'Farrell, the school cook. She was laughing already before she went through the door. Mrs O'Farrell was the kind of lady who laughed most of the time. Then while she was in there, everybody could hear her laughing and screaming. When she came out, she had to lean on the wall because she was laughing so much. 'Oh dear!' she gasped. 'That's the best twenty pence worth I've ever had. Oh dear me!'

She must have told a lot of people about it, because soon there was a long queue of very jolly people waiting to go in and lots of laughing and screaming coming from inside.

Nobody was really frightened by the Spooky Room. It was just a lot of fun, really, and lots of people thought it was clever, and very funny to see some of the children dressed up and jumping out to frighten them. 'Makes a change from a bottle stall, anyway!' said Mrs Williamson, the chair of the governors.

A spooky summer fair

When all the money was added up at the end of the day, Mr Deacon found that they had taken nearly £80 (£78.80 in fact) and a couple of foreign coins. That meant nearly 400 people had been through the Spooky Room.

✦ Conclusion

People enjoyed being frightened in the Spooky Room.

Do you think that you can really enjoy being frightened?

Can anyone think of a time when it's fun to be frightened?

Take some examples, eg. when a friend wears a halloween costume, when someone jumps out from behind a door or when they hear a scary story.

It's not like really being frightened is it? There's a big difference between being scared for fun and being scared for real. When something scares us for fun, we know it can't really hurt us, so we can be frightened and yet laugh at the same time.

Being really frightened, though, is not something to laugh about. Here are some things that we find really frightening and not at all funny.

- Being lost.
- Being in the dark in a strange place.
- Unexplained loud noises.
- Fierce animals.
- War and shooting.

All over the world, there are children who are really frightened most of the time. They are not in a Spooky Room having a laugh. They are in places where there is fighting – in Afghanistan or Israel, perhaps, or some of the African countries. They hear guns and shouting, people are hurt around them and their homes are attacked. Some of these children are alone because they have lost their parents.

Think what it must be like to be surrounded by strangers, all shouting and fighting, and to have lost your family – your parents and perhaps your brothers and sisters too. You don't know where they are or whether you will see them again.

Now and again, when we're frightened for fun or by something not very serious, let's think of the many children all over the world who are truly afraid most of the time.

A prayer

Dear God, we thank you for the changing seasons as they move across the face of the Earth. We remember the good times of summer and we look forward to the light that will be brought into our lives by the great festivals of Diwali and Christmas. Help us to remember the messages of those festivals – of the power of good to drive out evil and of the power of light to conquer the darkness in the world. Amen.

A thought

Laughter is close to tears. Sometimes you laugh and then it turns into crying. Sometimes you cry and it turns into laughter. Fear and fun are close together. And yet real fear is not funny at all. Fear can protect us – it stops us from doing silly things. But too much fear is bad, and if we are too afraid of someone or something – in school, in our lives or in our homes – we should tell someone about it.

Don't trap animals

Assembly 2 of 4

This assembly is about the danger of throwing away rubbish which might hurt pets or wild creatures. The story focusses on a hedgehog caught up in the plastic connector that joins cans of drink together.

You will need

- the OHT provided and a pen
- a pack of canned drinks held together by the plastic connector
- a connector on its own.

Taken by ....

Date ....

Given to ....

Comments

- ....
- ....
- ....

✦ Introduction

Hold up the plastic connector.

What is this?

Hold up the pack of drinks so that they can be seen.

This should give it away.

Hold up the plastic connector again.

This is quite useful isn't it? Why is it useful?

Take suggestions, eg. it makes shopping easier – you can carry four cans of drink at once.

What is it made of? Plastic. Is it easy to break it? No.

Let someone try, but be careful about hurt hands (gloves might be a good idea).

It's very strong, because if it broke easily, then it might break while you were carrying the cans of drink.

This is a useful thing, but it can also be very dangerous.

Here's a story that shows you how dangerous it can be.

📖 Story

Carl and Gemma were playing in the garden.

They had made their own tent. Their mum had given them a sheet and then loosened off the clothes line so that it hung near to the ground. They had put the sheet over the clothes line and then slipped under the sheet so that it was like a tent.

Gemma was trying to look at a book, but it was getting a bit too dark. Carl was singing to himself and pretending to play the piano. It would soon be time to go in. Their mum would be calling them from the kitchen door.

Suddenly, Gemma put her book down. 'What's that?' she asked.

Carl kept on singing.

'Carl!' said Gemma. 'Shut up and listen will you?'

Don't trap animals

Carl stopped singing.

Then they both heard it. A really peculiar sound. A sort of grunting, snorting, shuffling and scuffling.

Make these noises – or something like them – if you think you can!

Grunt, snort, shuffle, scuffle it went.

Grunt, snort, shuffle, scuffle.

'What on earth is it?' said Carl.

'What's that?' asked Gemma.

Carl wasn't sure. 'I'm not going,' he said. 'It sounds like that dinosaur from *Jurassic Park*.'

'Oh come on,' said Gemma, and she left the tent.

Carl followed close behind her.

They stood out in the garden. It was getting dark now, and it wasn't all that easy to see.

They listened carefully. There it was again.

Grunt, snort, shuffle, scuffle.

Grunt, snort, shuffle, scuffle.

'It's coming from the bushes at the end of the garden,' whispered Carl.

They tiptoed towards the bushes, a little bit afraid. Gemma went first and Carl went behind, hanging on to Gemma's T-shirt.

They got to the bushes. The noise was quite loud now.

Grunt, snort, shuffle, scuffle.

Grunt, snort, shuffle, scuffle.

Carl wanted to fetch Mum, but Gemma was already reaching under the bushes. Gemma lifted up some of the leaves near to the ground, and there they saw a very sad sight.

Carl gasped. 'Look, Gemma, oh the poor thing!'

It was a hedgehog.

Once they had seen it they weren't afraid any more. They often had hedgehogs in the garden. Mum said it was good because they eat slugs and other things that are harmful to garden plants, but that Gemma and Carl were not to touch them.

This hedgehog, though, wasn't eating anything. This hedgehog was in a lot of trouble.

They could see that he was all tangled up in something, and he was really struggling to get free, making all sorts of breathless noises.

Gemma looked closer and said, 'It's something made of plastic. He's tangled up in it.'

'Let's fetch Mum now,' said Carl, and off he went to the house, shouting, 'Mum, Mum!'

The door flew open – their mum had heard Carl shout and thought something bad had happened. She came running out of the kitchen.

'What's the matter? Are you alright?' she asked.

'Quick, Mum!' panted Carl. 'Up here.'

Mum ran behind Carl up to the end of the garden. She saw the hedgehog and straightaway knew what to do.

She went into the garden shed and came out wearing a pair of thick gardening gloves and carrying a pair of scissors. She picked up the hedgehog and very carefully cut off the plastic that he was tangled up in.

She put the hedgehog down. 'Off you pop then!' she said, and the hedgehog ran off into the bushes.

Don't trap animals

Mum held up the piece of plastic. She asked, 'Can you see what this is, you two?'

They knew straightaway. It was one of those connectors that holds cans of drinks together.

'It could have killed him,' Mum said. 'Lots of small animals are killed by these things – sometimes they strangle them, sometimes they stop them from eating. Somebody threw this down at the edge of the road I expect, and he got tangled up in it.'

'We didn't throw it down,' said Carl.

'No,' said Mum. 'We put things like this in the wheelie bin. But some people just throw things like this on the ground. They wouldn't do it if they knew the trouble it could cause.'

'Perhaps we should tell everyone?' said Carl.

'Yes,' agreed Gemma. 'We could make a poster and put it up in the corner shop.'

'What a great idea,' said Mum. With that the hedgehog gave a little snuffle from the distance as if he agreed.

✦ Conclusion

Put up OHT provided.

This might be an idea for Gemma and Carl's poster don't you think? Can you think of any words to put on the poster? *Add suggestions to the OHT.*

✦ Optional activity

Read out the following poem

Nasty rubbish in the hedgerow
Nasty rubbish in the grass
Nasty rubbish in the woodlands
Where tiny creatures pass.

Throwaway things bring danger
To creatures that don't know
About the things that trap and tangle
In the pathways where they go.

So put your rubbish in the bin
Don't leave it lying around
Remember all the creatures
That live there on the ground

A prayer

Lord, Help us to remember that what we do can affect others and help us to be thoughtful. Look after all the animals and keep them safe. Amen.

A thought

So many things that are useful can also be dangerous. We must always think of the effects of what we do. That's what being thoughtful means.

Song suggestions

'Milk bottle tops and paper bags', *Someone's Singing Lord*, 17

'The tidy song', *Tinder Box*, 47

Optional follow up

- Ask the children to make posters similar to the one Carl and Gemma might have made.
- Talk with children about other kinds of litter that might hurt animals.
- Ask children for stories they know of animals being hurt like this.

Don't trap animals

Don't trap animals!

Giving assistance

Assembly 3 of 4

This assembly is a straightforward tale of a small child who dials 999 to help her mum. It reminds children of what to do when something like that happens.

You will need

- the OHT provided
- a telephone (optional).

Taken by ....

Date ....

Given to ....

Comments

- ....
- ....
- ....

Note for the teacher

This assembly deals with dialling for the emergency services. Be aware of the possibility of encouraging children to do it unnecessarily. Consider using it in the context of a general theme on safety, or when the issue has arisen in other ways.

✦ Introduction

This assembly is about a very young child who knew exactly what to do when her mum had an accident. You will learn what to do if you are ever in such a situation.

Put up the OHT provided and reveal only the numbers 999. Ask if anyone knows what is special about this group of numbers. Someone will know that it's what we dial on the telephone in an emergency.

On the OHT, reveal the picture of the phone with the finger touching the '9' button. (Someone may know that you can also use 112. Accept this, but don't dwell on it. You don't want to complicate the story.)

Bring a volunteer out to practise dialling 999. (Mime or use a phone if you have one.)

Sometimes people find that in an emergency they have to call 999. This is what happens.

First, dial 999. Make sure all pupils know that this means pressing the nine button three times. The word 'dial' can be misleading.

The person who answers will say, 'Emergency, which service?'

They ask that because they want to know whether you want the police, or an ambulance or the fire service (or the coastguard, if you are in a coastal area).

It doesn't matter if you don't know. What matters is that you tell the person the address where you are, and what's happened. They will keep talking to you. Just keep answering and trying to tell them what they want to know.

Here's a story about someone who knew what to do.

Giving assistance

Story

Jenny was playing in her bedroom when she heard a terrific bang and a clattering noise outside. She went to have a look and found that her mum had fallen down the stairs. She was lying down at the bottom, not moving.

Jenny was a bit frightened, but she knew what to do because her mum had told her lots of times, and she had been told at school.

She hurried downstairs. She had a look at her mum, then went straight down the hall to the phone. She picked up the phone and remembered what it was she had to do.

She found the number nine on the keypad, held the phone to her ear and pressed the number nine three times. Straightaway a voice answered, 'Emergency, which service?'

Now Jenny wasn't sure what that meant, so she didn't say anything for a moment. The lady on the phone spoke again. 'Hello! Can you hear me?' she said. Jenny just said 'Yes'.

The lady on the phone knew from Jenny's voice that she was a little girl. 'What's your name, darling?' she asked. Jenny answered, 'I'm Jenny, and my mum has fallen downstairs. I think she's hurt herself.'

'Where do you live?' asked the lady.

Now Jenny knew her address very well. Her mum had taught her to say her address, so she said, '73 Dodwell Street, Nottingham.'

The operator now had enough information to be able to send an ambulance to the house. But she kept Jenny on the phone.

'Is your mum moving at all?' she said. Jenny had a quick look. 'No,' said Jenny.

'Is she breathing properly. Just go and put your face near her mouth and see if you can feel her breath. Come back and tell me.'

Jenny went over to her mum and bent down. She could feel her mum's breath on her face, and she could hear her making a sort of snoring noise. She went back to the phone.

'She's breathing. She's snoring a bit,' she said.

'Now, Jenny,' said the lady on the phone. 'When the ambulance comes, the paramedics will have to get into the house. Will you be able to let them in do you think?'

Jenny had a think about that. She thought about the latch on the inside of the front door. She knew it was too high for her.

So she said to the lady, 'I don't know.'

The lady said, 'Don't worry, Jenny. But when the men knock, stand away from the door, because they might have to bump against it to open it.'

But Jenny was still thinking about the latch. She shut her eyes and said a little prayer. 'Please help me to know what to do,' she said.

Then she had an idea. She went and got a chair and took it to the door. She stood on it and found that she could reach the latch and turn it. She pulled the door open just a bit. Then she got down and took the chair away from the door. She pulled the door open and looked out into the street. Just at that moment the ambulance turned the corner at the bottom of the street. It stopped at her door, and a man and a woman jumped out.

'Hello, love!' said the man. 'Shall we go in and see your mum?'

Jenny was very relieved that someone had come to help her. The two paramedics went to her mum and crouched down beside her. They spent quite a lot of time checking her and making sure she hadn't broken any bones. While they were doing that, her mum started to wake up. Suddenly she opened her eyes and saw the two strange people bending over her.

'Oh, oh, who are you?' she said. Then she stared around. 'Where's Jenny?' she asked.

The man said, 'We're paramedics, love. You've had a fall. Jenny's here. She's a good girl. She called 999 so we could come and help you.'

Then he called, 'Jenny! Come and see your mum. She's going to be OK.'

Jenny came and looked down at her mum. Her mum lifted her hand and held Jenny's hand and smiled. 'I always knew you were a good girl, Jenny. Well done.'

The paramedic said, 'We've got to take your mum to hospital now, Jenny, just to make sure she's OK. You can come too.'

Jenny's mum had to stay in for one night just to make sure she was alright. The next day she came home. She was really proud of Jenny, and she told all her friends, and one day a reporter and a photographer came and she was in the local paper. They made a fuss of her at school, too, and the headteacher gave her a special headteacher's certificate.

Jenny knew what to do. She didn't panic. Could you do that? I think you could.

✦ Conclusion

Do you all know how to dial 999? Look at the picture of the keypad. Can you all see the nine? Let's all pretend the keypad is on our knee, and we'll all press 999. Here goes.

Now let's make sure we all know our own address? Do you know it? Let's all say our addresses together, when I say one, two, three, go. It will be a real mixture of sounds. Come on then, one, two, three, go!

If you don't know it, don't worry. Practise it at home, or ask your teacher to help you. It's good to know your address, not just for dialling 999, but if you get lost and a police officer wants to help you. Try to learn it if you can.

Being small and young doesn't mean that you can't help people. Jenny didn't need strength to call 999. She just needed to remember the things she had been told.

A prayer

Lord, help us to know what to do when things go wrong. Be with us and keep us calm and help us to remember the things that we already know. Keep all our families from harm, and protect all the paramedics and hospital workers who help us when we are hurt or ill. Amen.

A thought

You can do lots of things. It's just remembering them at the right time that's sometimes difficult.

Song suggestions

When I needed a neighbour', *Someone's Singing Lord*, 35

'Family Prayer', *Primary Assembly Song Book*, 85

Giving assistance

999

Carpet children

Assembly 4 of 4

This assembly is about the exploitation of working children, exemplified by the story of Iqbal Masih, the former child carpet-worker who was murdered in 1995.

You will need

- the OHT provided.

Taken by ....

Date ....

Given to ....

Comments

- ....
- ....
- ....

Note for the teacher

The country with one of the worst records for the exploitation of child labour is Pakistan, and this is where most of the events in this assembly are centred. The country is not named, however, and you will need to be careful of provoking prejudicial reactions among children. In any case, no country is entirely free of the exploitation of children.

✦ Introduction

In our assembly today we're going to think about children all over the world who, instead of going to school, have to work very hard for very long hours to produce some of the goods that we buy without thinking very much about where they have come from.

In shops in the western world, you can buy beautiful carpets made in Eastern countries. How are these carpets made?

Akbar and Ashraf work in a carpet factory. They are eight and nine years of age. Every day they start work at six in the morning, and they go on until eight at night.

They are very skilled at their work. They make a very special kind of carpet that is created by knotting coloured thread onto a background of white threads. It can take Akbar and Ashraf six months to make one carpet, working many hours each and every day – knotting, knotting, knotting, all day long.

Do they enjoy their work? Would you? Of course they don't! It is boring, hard work that hurts and damages their young hands. Their master is cruel to them.

Akbar says, 'Staying here any longer fills me with dread. My parents are far away and all my friends are in school. My brother and I would like to be with our family. We would like to play with our friends. That is how children should live.'

Sadly, Akbar and Ashraf's father can't bring them home even if he wanted to. When they were very young he signed a paper allowing the owner of the carpet factory to take the boys away to his factory to work. In return the

Carpet children

owner gave their father some money. Their father was desperate for money to feed the other members of his family, and he could see no other way of doing it.

Reading

Very many children in Akbar and Ashraf's country work in bad conditions. They make many things as well as carpets.

Let me tell you about a factory where they make soccer balls. The balls are made by children aged between five and ten. They work for 80 hours a week. They have one half-hour break each day.

Do they chat to each other as they work? Do they sing to the radio, like the people who work in factories in Britain sometimes do?

No. The worst thing is that these children are made to keep completely silent, and the factory is kept almost completely dark. This is to make the boys concentrate on their work. There is a punishment room where children who do not work hard enough are beaten.

Many of these working children fall ill. Many of them sadly die while they are still young. But the good news is that there are good people who are trying to put things right – trying to convince the Government to change, trying to get people in other countries not to buy the things made by children.

One of the heroes of the struggle to free the working children was a little boy called Iqbal Masih.

Put up the OHT provided.

Iqbal started work in a carpet factory at the age of four. Then, when he was ten, some of the people who were trying to help the working children helped Iqbal to escape. He began to work with them, trying to get the law changed. He spoke at meetings all over the world, persuading people to be careful what they bought, and not to buy things made by child labour.

In America he appeared on television and visited schools, making young people think about what he stood for.

Then, on Easter Sunday 1995, Iqbal was shot dead while visiting relatives in a village near his home.

His death was a tragedy, but it really made people think. Now, most shops try not to buy goods made by children working in factories. If no one buys the goods, then the factories will close and the children will be free. Or if the factories do not close, they will have to employ adult workers and pay them proper wages.

Do not be afraid to talk about where the things used in school come from. Who made the soccer balls that you play with? Were they made in clean, healthy places, by adults free to come and go? Or were they made by slave children, the same age as you, in darkness and misery?

Ask the same question when you buy a soccer ball for yourself. Speak up. Think of Iqbal and the other children. Ask the same questions about your trainers, and the clothes you wear.

Around the world, two hundred million children aged between five and fifteen are exploited in dangerous working conditions.

✦ Conclusion

Every religion teaches adults to love, respect and care for children – not just the children in their own families, but all children. It is a sacred duty. But it is a rule that is broken every day by careless, selfish or greedy people. Iqbal showed that there are times when children should be prepared to have courage and speak up for themselves. So remember to ask about that soccer ball, and that pair of trainers.

A few years ago, Iqbal Masih visited Broad Meadows Middle School, in Quincy, USA. The students were deeply impressed with him, and very shocked when they heard he had been killed. They started a campaign to build a school in Iqbal's home region. And they have this advice to give to all of us.

'Shoppers must ask before buying, *Who* made the product? If enough shoppers ask that question enough times, it will show that shoppers care about the workers who made that product. Silence means agreement. Raise your voice for poor working children in sweatshops *and* in *sweatfields*! Who picked that crop? Prove it wasn't children.

Sincerely,

The Student Leaders of The Kids Campaign to Build a School for Iqbal'

A prayer

Lord, be with all children who have to work to earn money and food for their families. Give them hope and courage, and the knowledge of your love. Keep them in the minds of those who make decisions about the future of the world. Amen.

A thought

Earning a bit of pocket money sounds like a good idea. Freedom to go to school, to love your family and enjoy the company of your friends are also good ideas.

Song suggestions

'A perfect world', *Primary Assembly Song Book*, 61

'When I needed a neighbour' *Someone's Singing Lord*, 35

Optional follow up

Write to the campaign for Iqbal at Broad Meadows Middle School, Quincy, MA 02169, USA.

Look at the website. http://www.mirrorimage.com/iqbal

Alternatively, pick some of the common objects used in school, and try to track down where and how they were made.

Carpet children

A windy day

Assembly 1 of 4

You might use this assembly on a windy spring day, when the wind is obviously making noises and having an effect on the surroundings.

You will need

- OHT 1 provided on page 148
- OHT 2 provided on page 149
- an instrument – a wind chime if possible, if not, a metallophone or glockenspiel and a beater.

Taken by ....

Date ....

Given to ....

Comments

- ....
- ....
- ....

✦ Introduction

Let's listen to the wind for a while.

What sorts of sounds is it making?

On OHT 1 provided write any suggestions, eg. moaning through gaps in windows and doors.

Sometimes people let the wind make musical sounds, by putting instruments in the path of the wind.

The Greek God Hermes, it is said, had the empty shell of a tortoise that made lovely sounds when the wind blew through it.

Some African people put palm leaves in the path of the wind and the wind sings through them.

Some people make or buy wind chimes which tinkle and make lovely sounds when the wind blows.

These are some wind chimes.

Show OHT 2 and blow on the wind chime or play the metallophone/glockenspiel.

We can't see the wind, but we can see what it does, and we can hear it blowing round the buildings, through the doors and windows and through the trees and bushes. Sometimes it bangs doors and windows.

Here's a story about the mischievous wind.

🕮 Story

'Hooray!' cried the wind. 'I'll have a good game today!'

And the wind set out on a swooping, gusty, racing journey over the land.

It could hardly wait to scatter leaves, bang doors and windows and generally cause a great deal of irritation and annoyance.

'Aren't I strong and clever!' called out the wind as it blasted through the park gates.

It bent the newly-planted trees at the park entrance so hard that they were nearly at the point of breaking.

'Stop! Stop!' cried the gardener. 'These sapling trees will break. Leave them alone!'

A windy day

But the wind just laughed and blew harder still, so that the trees bent over until they nearly touched the ground.

Then it relented and crossed the park to the pond.

On the pond was a family of newly-hatched ducklings. The little ducklings squawked in alarm as their feathers ruffled up.

They were blown in all directions across the pond, the waves chasing them.

'Stop! Stop!' cried the mother duck. 'You are nearly blowing my little ducklings away! The big waves will drown them.'

But the wind just laughed and blew harder still so that the little ducklings became tired and frightened, and their mother had to gather them into the nest until the wind had passed.

By now, the wind had reached the far side of the park and had started to annoy the people who were out for walks.

It blew an old lady's hat off and made it roll right down the path.

It blew a man's umbrella inside out.

It nearly blew a little toddler right off her feet, and her mum had to hold on to her tightly.

'Stop! Stop!' said the toddler's mum. 'You will blow my baby off her feet.'

But the wind laughed and kept on blowing so that the toddler's cheeks were red and her mum had to cuddle her to stop her crying.

'My!' cried the wind. 'What a wonderful time I am having today.'

Then the wind swooped down on a row of shops.

It blew on the canopies over the shop windows and made them rattle.

It blew on the advertising boards outside the shops and knocked them over.

It blew on the florist's display of flowers and made the petals fly.

'Stop! Stop!' cried the florist. 'You will blow all my flowers to pieces and you will blow the canopy off my shop!'

But the wind laughed and kept on blowing so that all the shopkeepers had to run to put their canopies away and bring their displays inside.

Then the wind headed for a garden next to the park.

'I'll have good fun here!' said the wind. And the wind blew hard in the garden to see what confusion might be caused.

But there was no confusion. Instead, what the wind heard was a wonderful sound – a lovely, heavenly, chiming sound, like little bells.

Blow gently on the wind chime or play the metallophone/glockenspiel slowly and quietly.

'What is that?' said the wind. 'I'll blow louder and stop that sound.'

But instead of the sound stopping, the more the wind blew, the more the chiming went on.

Blow stronger or play a little quicker and louder.

In the house, a lady pulled back the curtains and looked out.

'Listen!' she said to her children. 'The wind is blowing, and making lovely sounds from the wind chimes hanging in the apple tree. The wind makes some rough sounds and it annoys some people. But it doesn't annoy us, because the more it blows, the more beautiful the sounds from our wind chimes.'

And out in the garden the wind blew and blew, and the wind chimes played and played their beautiful song.

Blow more and more gently or play more and more quietly. Finish with a moment of silence.

✦ Conclusion

The wind can be very mischievous. In storms it can be so powerful that it can pull trees up and blow down houses.

Fortunately that doesn't happen very often though. More often, we use wind to help us.

It can fill the sails of boats to power them across oceans. Windmills have been used for many hundreds of years to gather the wind's strength and use it to turn machinery.

If we get scared by the noises the wind makes or the way it seems to sweep us off our feet, we can remember how useful it can be and how it can make very beautiful music.

A prayer

Dear God, we thank you for the gifts of the weather. For the warming sun to cheer us up. For the rain to wash the streets and make our countryside green. For the snow to make the land magical and white. For wind to carry the seeds of plants and trees far around and to make us feel excited. Amen.

A thought

In some countries, the weather is much the same every day for long periods of time. People who go from Britain to countries like that often miss our weather and the way it changes. It can be quite boring to have the same weather every day, even if the sun shines a lot. We are lucky to have a good mixture of rain and sunshine to keep the countryside green.

Song suggestions

'Who has seen the wind?', *Tinder Box*, 44

'It's a bright and breezy day', *Primary Assembly Song Book*, 6

Optional follow up

- Build up a sound story of the journey of the wind using percussion instruments.
- Discuss the use of natural power – sun, waves and wind.

A windy day

The sounds of the wind

A Windy Day

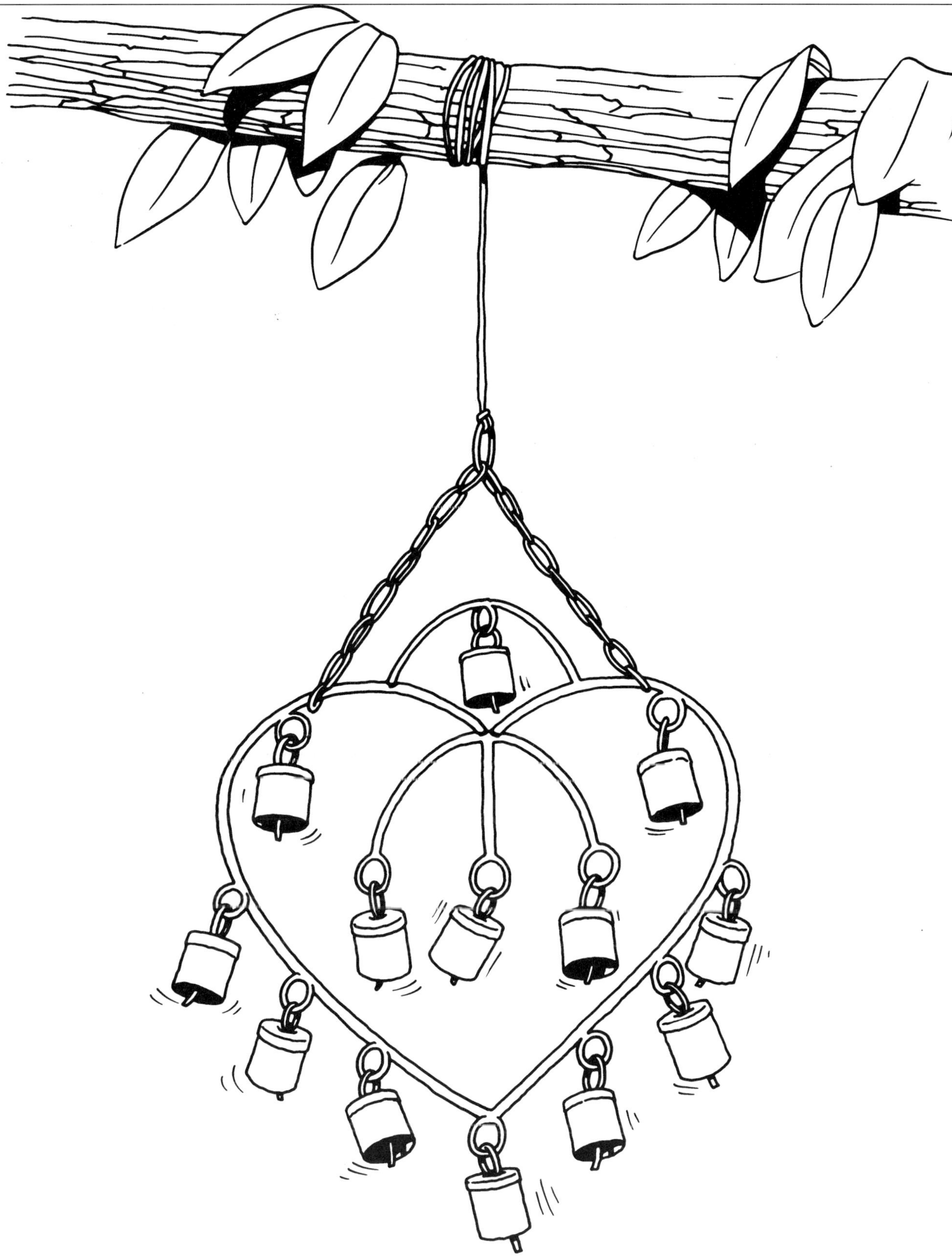

A windchime

It's about so big

Assembly 2 of 4

This assembly looks at how we can explain to others about the size and shape of objects without measuring them exactly. It is also about how living things need to be cared for and nurtured in order to thrive and develop to full potential.

You will need

- a sunflower seed.

Taken by ....

Date ....

Given to ....

Comments

- ....
- ....
- ....

✦ Introduction

This assembly is about size and how things grow. It marvels at what can be produced from a tiny seed and compares this to how we grow from babies to adults.

My Uncle Jim's favourite hobby was fishing and whenever he had spare time, he'd take his fishing rod and some bait down to the canal near his home.

He had a small stool that unfolded and he'd sit there watching the tip of the float bobbing gently in the water.

I don't know whether he caught any fish, because he didn't take any home.

Whenever I called to see him, he'd tell me about the enormous fish he'd once caught.

He would say, 'It was so big *(exaggerate size!)*. I couldn't have carried it home, so I put it back in the water.'

How big do you think my Uncle Jim's fish was? Take care not to bump the person next to you, and you can all show me how big it was.

It was bigger than your head. Smaller than a car. Bigger than a mouse. Smaller than a camel. Bigger than a guinea pig. Smaller than my front door.

When we want to say how big or small something is, we often do it by comparing it with something else.

Now what do you think is in my hand?

Hold up your hand with the sunflower seed hidden in it.

It's got to be fairly small, hasn't it?

Shake your hand.

Can you hear it?

Hold your hand to your ear.

I can't hear any sound at all.

Hold the sunflower seed in your fingers and show it.

There, who can tell us what it is now?

Yes, it's a sunflower seed. It's not very big and it doesn't look very exciting.

Let's hear a story about it.

Story

Sarah and her twin brother Richard loved going to see their gran and grandpa.

They lived in the same road and Sarah and Richard used to pop in on their way home from school.

Gran always had a drink and a special home-made biscuit waiting for them. She would always say, 'Now don't let that spoil your appetite!'

Gran and Grandpa had a beautiful garden, and whatever the time of year, it was full of colour and interesting things. It was their pride and joy.

There was a rich, green lawn that Grandpa cut with the mower so that it made lines up and down. Richard used to stride up and down the lines like a giant walking home for his tea.

'Fourteen, fifteen strides today, Gran, that's the lowest yet!' exclaimed Richard one day. 'Last time it was sixteen and last year it was twenty.'

'I'll put it on your chart,' said Gran and she wrote it down on a piece of paper that was pinned to the inside of the shed door.

The shed had that special gardening smell and it was full of gardening tools, boxes and bags of compost for growing plants. It was quite cosy too and the twins loved to sit on the tall stools and look out across the garden.

The sides of the shed were as tall as Grandpa and it had a pointy roof where the pigeons perched. On a wooden shelf against the window were small plant pots.

'What's in this, Gran?' asked Sarah, noticing a bright, yellow pot with a label on it.

'Oh that's special that is. It's going to grow taller than you in a few week's time.'

'Is it the beanstalk that Richard the giant came down?' laughed Sarah. Richard gave her one of his looks.

'Why's it special, Gran? I can't see anything except black compost,' added Richard.

Gran started to explain, 'Well, every year the Council organises a competition to see who can grow the tallest sunflower and Grandpa and I thought we'd have a go this year. We've got a sunflower seed each.'

'Last year's winner was as tall as this shed,' said Grandpa.

'That's about as big as you and Sarah put together, but we're hoping to grow ours even taller,' said Gran.

'Look,' said Grandpa, taking a seed carefully out of the packet. 'That's how big they are to start with.'

'Wow!' gasped Richard. 'It's the size of my fingernail.'

He looked closely at the sunflower seed that Grandpa had put on the palm of his hand. 'Our gerbil has these seeds in its food – it's not going to grow as big as me and Sarah is it?'

'No, of course not,' reassured Gran. 'The seed has to have the right conditions to grow – warmth and light and lots of love and care.'

 ISBN 1 874050 55 4

It's about so big

'How about you two planting this sunflower seed, then you can look after it and watch it grow?' Grandpa asked the twins.

'Oh yes, please!' Sarah and Richard replied together.

So they planted their sunflower seed and put a label on the plant pot with their names and the date when they planted it.

Over the next weeks, the twins looked after their sunflower and watched it grow. At first the shoot was only about as tall as your little finger, but soon it was the length of a pencil.

Grandpa said it needed planting out in a special part of the garden that was sheltered from the wind, but also got lots of warmth from the sun.

Gradually the sunflower grew taller and stronger with large leaves the size of dinner plates.

Then a wonderful flower started to open, a beautiful, round flower with lots of petals. At first it was only small, about as big as the twins' birthday badges. Then it was like a saucer, until eventually it was the size of a frisbee.

Every day when the sun shone, the sunflower turned its head towards it.

Finally came the day when the man from the Council came to measure the sunflower for the competition.

The sunflower had grown so tall that it was given the first prize. They were presented with a certificate and a photograph in a beautiful frame which Mum said would look perfect in the living room by the window, to remind them of the sunflower that grew taller than Grandpa's shed.

✦ Conclusion

It's hard to imagine that an enormous plant, taller than Grandpa's shed, could grow from such a small, uninteresting seed the size of a fingernail.

A seed the size of your fingernail. A flower as big as a frisbee. Leaves the size of dinner plates. A sunflower taller than Grandpa's shed.

We can describe the size of things without measuring them. For example, once when I bumped my head, a lump came up that was as big as a conker. I couldn't measure the bump precisely, so I described the size compared to something else.

The twins were able to explain the size of various things in the story without actually measuring them because they knew the size compared to something else.

Measuring things exactly isn't always easy and sometimes we just don't have the right equipment. So to be able to compare it to something else that people can understand is very useful.

Hold up the sunflower seed again.

Look again at the sunflower seed.

All this tiny seed needs to grow into a wonderful plant as tall as a shed are the right conditions – warmth, light, water, love and care.

We're very similar to seeds, aren't we? We're very small when we're born and need lots of looking after. Think of a baby – small enough to rest on my forearm, a head the size of my hand. But just look how you've all grown since you were babies and you're still growing!

A prayer

Dear God, thank you for our gardens and all living things, for the sun and rain to help the plants to grow. We are all part of a family and we need each other's love and care to help us to grow strong in mind and body. Amen.

A thought

Just as the twins very carefully looked after the sunflower seed as it grew, so our families and friends are very helpful and caring with us as we grow. We need food, water and shelter, but we also need love.

Song suggestions

'A wonderful thing', *Primary Assembly Song Book*, 32

'The flowers that grow in the garden', *Someone's Singing Lord*, 53

Optional follow up

- Each class can plant and look after a sunflower seed. Measure it and keep a record.

What's a rainbow?

Assembly 3 of 4

As adults we commonly find awe and wonder in nature. Children, though, are discovering it for the first time, and this assembly helps them to see the lifetime effect that a common natural spectacle can have. In the story, a child sees a very clear rainbow. The child understands it is a common enough scientific phenomenon, but a wonderful sight nevertheless.

You will need

- nothing at all.

Taken by ....

Date ....

Given to ....

Comments

- ....
- ....
- ....

✦ Introduction

In this assembly we'll see just how wonderful are some of the sights and experiences around us, each one a witness to the power of nature and the presence of God.

The sky is always changing. Sometimes there are white clouds, sometimes there is only blue sky and sunshine. Sometimes there are only dark clouds and rain.

But just sometimes you can see the most beautiful thing that comes into the sky. I mean the rainbow. It appears when there is both rain and sunshine, and the sun can shine on falling rain. Of all the wonderful things of nature, the rainbow is one of the most beautiful to look at.

In this story, a grown-up person remembers the day she saw a rainbow when she was in the playground at school. It is a memory not just of something that she saw, but of the feelings she had at that time, and of the people that she shared the day with.

📖 Story

I remember the day our teacher showed us a rainbow. It was one of those days when it can't make up its mind whether it's a fine day or a rainy day.

Then at playtime the rain came just at the wrong moment. A big, black cloud appeared and there was a sudden heavy shower. One of the teachers came out and blew a whistle and all the teachers and classroom assistants hurried out to bring us in.

After break, the teachers settled everyone down, as the rain shower continued outside.

It was then that our teacher, Miss Hofkins, straightened up from the table where she was helping one of the groups, and walked over to the window. 'Come and look at this,' she said. 'Look at this beautiful rainbow. Quick, let's go outside and get a better look.'

I remember it so well. She said, 'Quickly, children – quickly, no pushing, we're going outside. Be sensible now.'

What's a rainbow?

And there, out in the playground, Miss Hofkins pointed to the rainbow. I suppose I must have seen one before, but I really don't remember. What was special was being in our playground, and Miss Hofkins pointing to the rainbow. I can see the scene still in my mind. I looked around and there were all these little faces looking up and pointing, and Miss Hofkins, one hand holding her hair, because it was blowing a bit in the wind, and the other hand pointing upwards. And her face turned to us, with a big, beautiful smile.

It was the most beautiful rainbow. It was very clear and complete – a strong arch across the sky, with all the colours on display. Miss Hofkins got us to say all the colours with her. Red, orange, yellow, green, blue, indigo and violet.

I remember that I wasn't sure how to say indigo, and I wasn't certain I could see a difference between indigo and violet, or between orange and yellow. But it didn't matter. It was such a beautiful rainbow, and I was content just to look at it.

I remember trying to see the end of it. The end seemed to come down on the other side of the bypass, beyond the houses, away in the countryside on the other side of some distant woods. I thought how good it would be to go to the end of the rainbow and stand among all those colours and be dazzled by the brightness.

Oh, how I longed to go there – just to walk into the distance, into the fields, and through the woods and out the other side. I thought I would come out of the woods and there just in front of me would be this wonderful sight of the rainbow coming down to the ground. I would walk into it, and be dazzled by the light and the colour, and I would be the person who went to the end of the rainbow.

Later on, of course, Miss Hofkins explained that you couldn't really get to the end of the rainbow, because it kept going away from you if you went towards it. All the same, I had this dream of being able to get there and find the magical spot where the rainbow reached the ground and turned everything into brightness and colour.

We watched the rainbow until it faded and the sun went in, and it got a little colder and the rain came again. Then we went inside, and Miss Hofkins told us some things about rainbows – how they come when there is rain and sunshine at the same time, and how the sun shines through the raindrops and the light of the sun is broken up into all the colours of the rainbow.

I've been all over the world since then, and I've seen rainbows over the ocean, and I've looked out of aeroplanes and seen rainbows in the clouds. I've even seen the rainbows in the spray at Niagara Falls, a big waterfall. But I'll never forget the rainbow I saw that day at school. I see in my mind's eye the rainbow dipping down across the fields beyond the distant woods, and I still feel the feeling I had then, how I longed to find the place where it ended and be bathed in its colour and light. Even though Miss Hofkins told me that I couldn't go to the rainbow's end, I still feel somehow that one day I might make it.

✦ Conclusion

The Bible has a story about a rainbow. In the book of Genisis, there is the story of Noah. Now Noah, you might remember, built an ark – Noah's ark – a big boat. Do you remember why he built it? He built it because God had decided to send a big flood all over the world, and he told Noah to build his ark so that he and his family would not drown in the flood. And do you remember what else had to come on the ark with Noah? He had to bring two of every kind of animal and bird, so that when the flood went down, the animals and birds would come out of the ark and replace all the animals that had been drowned in the flood.

They all went into the ark and it floated on the flood waters. Then when the floods went down, and they could all get onto the dry land again, God made a rainbow – he called it his 'bow in the cloud'. God said it was a sign – a promise that he would not flood the Earth again.

When a rainbow comes, take time to look at it. Look at the way the colours change. Look at where the rainbow ends, and try to imagine what it would be like to be there, even though you can never really get there.

The rainbow is a beautiful example of something that can be explained by science, but which tells us of God's love and of the beauty of his Earth.

A prayer

Lord, we thank you for the beauties of the Earth – for the rain and sun, and the rainbow, which is your promise to us of your love and care for us. Help us to protect your Earth and all the creatures and people that live on it. Amen.

A thought

A rainbow is just one of the many beautiful sights in the natural world. We only have to look around us to see how wonderful our world is.

Song suggestions

'To God who makes all lovely things', *Someone's Singing Lord* 9

'It's a bright and breezy day', *Primary Assembly Song Book* 6

Optional follow up

Draw or paint a rainbow. Add what you think you might find at the end of the rainbow.

The night sky

Assembly 4 of 4

In this assembly, a little girl encounters the awesome wonder of the night sky. When she sees it and reflects upon it, she starts to understand that the universe is vast and wonderful, and that to think about it can lessen some of our concerns and worries.

You will need

- nothing at all.

Taken by ....

Date ....

Given to ....

Comments

- ....
- ....
- ....

✦ Introduction

Who remembers what they saw on the way to school today?

That seems a strange question, but it isn't really. Because I think you saw lots of things that you can't now remember. Whether you were in a car, or walking, you would be thinking and talking, and all the time you would be seeing things and not really taking them in.

That's quite natural. Your mind works like that. It concentrates on one thing, and other things just sort of pass by without being noticed, unless something draws your attention to them.

One of the things that's always there, and is often quite wonderful to see, is the sky above our heads. Sometimes it's clear blue, sometimes it's dark and threatening, sometimes there are mountains of white cloud. The great artist, Constable, was always looking at the sky. He painted lots of pictures with just clouds in them, he tried hard to get them just right. And yet we walk around underneath the sky and hardly ever look up and think about the constantly changing beauty of the clouds.

At night, of course, if the sky is clear, we see the moon and the stars. Except that often we don't see them. The lights from our houses and shops and from the big lights by the side of the roads make it difficult to see into the sky at night. In our story today, Kathy sees the night sky clearly for the first time, and thinks about how small she and her problems seem by comparison.

🕮 Story

Every year, Mr Chadwick took Year 2 children to stay in the countryside at a hostel that belonged to the church. They were quite young to go on a trip away from home, but the hostel was quite close, and homely, and Mr Chadwick and the parents thought it was a good opportunity for the children to have the experience of sleeping away from home.

 ISBN 1 874050 55 4

The night sky

Although the hostel was not far, it was out of town, and you had to go there by coach, so it seemed like a big adventure.

The children in Reception and Year 1 really looked forward to being in Year Two so they could go to the hostel with Mr Chadwick. And then when they were in Year Two, they looked forward to the time when they could go on the trip.

St Martin's wasn't a very big school, and usually about twenty children went. The parents were always a bit anxious, because hardly any of the children had been away from home before, and the parents were always worried that their children would be upset and want to come home.

Kathy's mum kept saying to Kathy, 'Now you'll be alright, won't you? You won't worry, will you?' And Kathy kept saying, 'I'll be alright Mum, really.'

Then came the big day. The coach came up the road, and the children filed out with Mr Chadwick. The parents came along to see everyone off. Then there was a lot of waving and blowing kisses and the coach pulled away.

It wasn't far to the hostel. Out of town, along the main road for a while and down some country lanes. The hostel was a big old house. It was a bit shabby really, in need of some paint and some new furniture. But it was clean and it smelled of polish.

Kathy and seven other girls slept in a room with eight beds, four on each side of the room. Mr Chadwick said that when a rich family lived in the house, long ago, it had been one person's bedroom.

Mrs Chadwick, two of the parents and a classroom assistant had come along with Mr Chadwick to help, and the adults stayed with the children and helped them to unpack their things.

After tea, everyone played rounders in the grounds. Then they gathered under a tree and Mr Chadwick read some stories. And they all just talked about the stories and about what they were going to be doing for the rest of their time there.

'We're only here for two full days,' said Mr Chadwick. 'So we'll make the most of them.' Then he said something mysterious. He looked up at the sky and said, 'And tonight I think there will be a special treat.'

Everyone wondered what that could be.

Soon it was dark, and everyone went inside and sat around in the lounge playing board games and reading.

And that was the moment that Kathy suddenly got upset.

She looked at the dark outside, and she looked around at the big room with oak panelled walls, and she thought about her little house with her mum singing in the kitchen, and a big tear came into her eye and rolled down her cheek. 'I wish I was at home,' she said to herself.

Mrs Chadwick was keeping a careful eye on everyone, and she noticed that Kathy was upset, and she came over.

'Feeling a bit homesick, Kathy?' she asked, and Kathy nodded.

Mrs Chadwick didn't tell her off or tell her to pull herself together. She just said, 'That's quite natural Kathy. Everyone feels a bit homesick when they first go away from home, even for a day. I still miss my home when I come away. Mind you, I do like being with all you lovely children.'

Mrs Chadwick sat and talked to Kathy and made her laugh a bit, and got some of the other children to gather round while they chatted. Then Mr Chadwick came in.

'Listen everyone,' he said. 'I told you we were going to have a special treat, and it's time for that now. I want you to get your coats and line up by the front door.'

'Going outside, are we?' thought Kathy. 'I don't know if I'll like that, not in the dark.' And she started to feel upset again.

The children lined up, and Mr Chadwick went off at the front and led everyone out of the house, round the back to the end of the garden, and onto a little path that led from the garden into some woods.

'Keep up, everyone,' called Mr Chadwick. He was walking at the front with a torch, and Mrs Chadwick was at the back making sure nobody got left behind.

The path led through the trees. It was a bit spooky really, and Kathy wasn't at all sure that she liked it.

The other children kept squealing and saying that they could see ghosts and tigers, but nobody really believed them.

Then the path started to go uphill. Up and up it climbed, higher and higher. Everyone was puffing and blowing, and Mr Chadwick was striding on and saying, 'Come on, everyone, keep going.'

Then, quite suddenly, they all came out from the trees and into a clear space that was just grass. The trees were around, but there was only the sky above now.

'Right,' said Mr Chadwick. 'Now come to the middle of this clearing and look up.'

That's what they did. And there was the night sky – the stars, as clear as anything, hundreds, no, thousands of them. It was breathtaking and everyone went very quiet.

'We've never seen the stars before,' said Kathy to Mr Chadwick. 'Not properly like this.'

'No,' said Mr Chadwick. 'In town you don't see them, because the street lights and the lights in the buildings shine too brightly and you can't see past them into the sky. So the stars are there, but they aren't so easy to see in town. Here, though, we can see them. And because the sky is clear and the moon isn't out, it's even better.'

Then he said, 'The grass is dry. Let's sit or lie on the grass and just look up and enjoy the stars.'

So that's what they did. It was a wonderful sight. Kathy had never realised that there were so many stars, all crowded together. And across the sky was an area where there were even more – so many that it looked almost like a cloud.

'Can you see the Milky Way, everyone?' said Mr Chadwick. 'Where there are more stars than anywhere else.'

Kathy looked. She felt overwhelmed by it all. As if she was looking deep into endless space, millions and millions of miles out into the universe.

Her eyes roamed across the great array of stars. She wondered what they were like when

 ISBN 1 874050 55 4

The night sky

you got nearer to them. Were they bright like the sun? Were there planets out there, with people on them. Was there someone lying on a grassy hill on another world, millions of miles away, looking out and wondering about life in other places?

It was a breathtaking thought. Suddenly, Kathy realised that her homesickness had quite gone. Out there, the universe seemed so big and majestic that it didn't seem right to have little feelings like homesickness. This Earth was her home, after all, and it felt comfortingly solid against her back as she looked into the depths of endless space.

Then Mr Chadwick said, 'Be quiet everyone, while I say a prayer.'

'Dear Lord,' he said. 'We praise you for the beauty of the night sky. We think of children all over the world looking up at them and sharing them with us.

'We think of all the people since the beginning of time who have looked up at these same stars. And we think of all the people in the many years to come who will look at them.

'Your universe is bigger and more wonderful than we can imagine. We are small by comparison, but you know we are here.

'We ask you to be with us as we enjoy our time together these two days. Amen.'

Everyone said amen, and then Mr Chadwick stood up and everyone started off down the hill again. Kathy walked at the back with Mrs Chadwick. 'Feeling better now, Kathy?' asked Mrs Chadwick.

Kathy nodded. 'Yes thank you,' she said. 'Seeing those stars and thinking about God made me feel a lot better.'

✦ Conclusion

Try to take notice of the wonderful things that we sometimes take for granted – the beauty of the clouds or the trees. And when you see them, take a little time just to think that even though we see them every day, they are still wonderful examples of nature and of God's creation. If you like, you can say a little prayer of thankfulness from time to time for the beauty of the created world around us.

A prayer

Lord, we thank you for the world and the universe in which we live. Help us never to take it for granted. Help us to use the beauty we see around us to remind us of you and of our duty to look after the world that you have made. Amen.

A thought

It's important to stop and look at things properly sometimes – if you do that you can have new thoughts about familiar things.

Song suggestions

'God who put the stars in space', *Someone's Singing Lord* 47

'Somebody greater', *Come and Praise* 5

Optional follow up

Make a list of the natural things that you see on the way to school – do you see trees? Think carefully about where they are. Flowers? The sky? Go over the route carefully and you might be surprised how many things appear on your list.